MENTAL HEALTH & MURDER

Understanding The Darkness
That Consumed My Sister

JOE HASTINGS

Copyright © 2024 Joe Hastings

All Rights Reserved

Mount Juliet, Tennessee USA

ISBN: 979-8-9920982-0-4 (PaperBack)

ISBN: 979-8-9920982-1-1 (ePub)

ISBN: 979-8-9920982-3-5 (Hard Cover)

Library of Congress Control Number: 2024925305

No part of this publication may be reproduced, distributed, or transmitted in any form or by any means, including photocopy, recording, or other mechanical methods, without prior written permission of the publisher, except as permitted by U.S. copyright law. For permission requests, contact: AuthorJoeHastings.com

This book is memoir. It reflects the author's present recollections of experiences over time. Some names and characters have been changed, some events have been compressed, and some dialogue may have been recreated.

The author has made every attempt to provide information that is accurate and complete, but this book is not intended as a substitute for professional medical advice. This book is not meant to be used, nor should it be used, to diagnose or treat any medical or psychological condition. Readers are advised to consult their own medical advisors whose responsibility it is to determine the condition of, and best treatment for, the reader.

First Edition

Printed in the USA

ACKNOWLEDGMENTS

First and foremost, I want to thank my wife. Your unwavering support, love, and extreme patience have been my anchor throughout this journey. You've stood by me through every high and low, and for that, I am eternally grateful. I couldn't have done this without you.

A special thank you to Shelley Jones, LICSW, for your invaluable insight and expertise in mental health. Your guidance helped me navigate and better understand the complexities of mental illness, bringing clarity to some of its most difficult aspects.

To my sister, Angelee. Your presence in my life and this story means more to me than words can express. I love you.

Lastly, to everyone who has faced challenges with mental health, whether personally or by supporting a loved one—this book is for you. I hope it serves as a reminder that you are not alone.

A NOTE TO THE READER

This book contains sensitive and potentially triggering material. It includes explicit accounts of murder, animal deaths, and a struggle with untreated mental illness that leads to tragedy. There are descriptions of violent scenes and acts, emotionally intense moments of grief and shock, and references to suicide. If you or someone you know is affected by mental health issues, please read with care and seek support if needed.

While the core of Parts III and IV remain grounded in the facts of the case, they've been written in a fictionalized narrative style. My goal was to expand beyond the courtroom's stark realities and immerse you in the vivid, often haunting images that formed in my mind as I sat through the testimony. My hope is that this style helps you feel the weight of those moments as deeply as I did.

TABLE OF CONTENTS

Acknowledgments iii
A Note to the Reader v
Preface 1
Introduction 5

PART I: WAY BACK WHEN 7

Chapter 1: A Daughter Long Dreamed Of 9
Chapter 2: Chaos Beneath the Surface 15
Chapter 3: Caged In The Shack 23
Chapter 4: A Father Returns 29
Chapter 5: Shattered Roots 33
Chapter 6: A Stage Full of Dreams 37
Chapter 7: Going Full Circle 43
Chapter 8: Dandelions in the Dark 49
Chapter 9: The Weight of the World 55
Chapter 10: The Shifting Sands of Stability 59
Chapter 11: Rediscovering Dreams 63
Chapter 12: Mom's Death and the Aftermath 67
Chapter 13: The Day My World Changed Forever 75
Chapter 14: The Road to Uncertainty 79
Chapter 15: A Family in Shadows 83
Chapter 16: Facing the Darkness 89

PART II: THE HEARING 95

Chapter 17: A Sister in Chains 97

Chapter 18: My Current Mindset 101

Chapter 19: Buckle Up 105

Chapter 20: A Crash, Tyvek and Bombshells 109

Chapter 21: First Responder's Testimony 113

Chapter 22: The Ambulance Ride 117

Chapter 23: Bearing the Burden 123

Chapter 24: Signals of Distress 127

PART III: AT THE HOSPITAL 129

Chapter 25: Whispers of Madness 131

Chapter 26: Blood-Stained Realities 137

Chapter 27: Inside the Storm 141

Chapter 28: The Bloodbath 147

Chapter 29: Beneath the Blood 153

PART IV: SCENE OF THE CRIME 157

Chapter 30: The Frozen Truth 159

Chapter 31: Shadows in the Snow 163

Chapter 32: A Heavy Silence 169

Chapter 33: Between Grief and Compassion 173

Chapter 34: The Final Examination 179

Chapter 35: Layers of Pain 183

Chapter 36: The Anatomy of Violence 187

Chapter 37: A Moment of Reflection 191

Chapter 38: Shattered Reality 195

Chapter 39: The Final Witness 201

Chapter 40: The 911 Call 205

Chapter 41: Closing Statement of The Prosecution 209

Chapter 42: Closing Statement of The Defense 213

Chapter 43: The Gavel Swings 215

Chapter 44: A Journey to Understanding 219

PART V 223

Chapter 45: Lost In Your Own Paranoia 225

Chapter 46: Living in a Simulation 229

Chapter 47: Driven by Delusions 233

The Final Chapter: Finding Light in the Shadows 239

About the Author 245

PREFACE

My sister killed a man. She killed two dogs. One gun laid on the kitchen counter, another on the floor by his body. A large butcher knife, covered in blood, was on the bed.

When I began writing, I had no intentions of creating a book. I was just trying to process all the emotions, feelings, and thoughts that had overwhelmed me since the tragic event occurred. I could hardly find the words to describe it. The act of violence my sister committed was so unimaginable that the news ripped through us, leaving me and my family shattered and heartbroken. My sister, the one I knew, had become someone I could no longer recognize. She had become someone who couldn't escape the demons in her own mind, capable of a horror nobody could have expected.

What began as a personal exercise gradually turned into something much, much more. I began to see that this story wasn't just about a tragic event; it was about everything leading up to it. The hidden struggle with mental illness, the signs we may have missed, and the unrelenting grip of trauma that altered the course of our lives.

It became obvious to me, realizing how much I felt this story needed to be told. Not just for my own healing, but for anyone who has been touched by mental illness in their lives. My hope is that by sharing our story, others may become more aware of the signs of mental illness. To recognize those struggles that so often go unnoticed until it's too late. The importance of mental health cannot be overstated here, period. My wish is that this book might inspire greater compassion and awareness towards those suffering in silence—and perhaps, help them find a way forward.

This book is a deeply personal reflection on my life with Angelee, beginning with our shared childhood along with the years we grew up together. It's told explicitly through my eyes, my memories, and my emotions. As you read, you'll experience our story as I lived it, shaped by the love, confusion, and heartbreak that only I can express.

Growing up, being resilient wasn't really a choice for us, it was a necessity that life demanded of us. Nothing came easily, and we quickly learned that survival meant fighting for every inch of life's comforts and stability. We scraped, we scrounged, and we endured, building strength, compassion, and determination. Even still, there was no amount of fortitude that could have ever prepared me for the moment I learned about the unspeakable act Angelee committed.

This story isn't just a recounting of events that have happened, it's my attempt to make sense of the senseless. Through the pages of this book, you'll witness the story unfold, as I lived it. You'll feel the pressure of each revelation and understand how these events have reshaped the memories I have of my sister. The love and joy we shared will always remain, but I now see them through a new lens, one marked by reflection and a deeper clarity I hadn't been able to understand before.

When I'm reflecting on the evidentiary hearing, I want to be clear as possible: this is not a word-for-word, factual recounting of the proceedings. Rather, it's my emotional journey, my attempt to process an experience that defies explanation. I want to share what it was like to sit in that courtroom, absorbing the words spoken and confronting my own feelings of disbelief and grief.

I understand that our memories can be fragile and are sometimes reshaped over time. There may be details that I may have missed or moments I might have misremembered, and for that, I sincerely apologize. Again, my goal is not to provide a factual record of the hearing, but to share a lived experience that was deeply emotional and fundamentally transformative. These are the thoughts and feelings that suffocated me as I tried to make sense of a world that had been irrevocably altered.

I need for this to be understood as well: there is no intention in my words to assign blame or shift responsibility. Nor am I trying to mislead anyone about the facts. I write this with the deepest respect for everyone involved, and I hope my words are received with the understanding and reflection they're meant to inspire. Respectfully, I have changed the names of all those involved, except Angelee and Bill.

Thank you for allowing me to share my story with you.

Joe

INTRODUCTION

The blood. There was so much blood. It was everywhere—smeared, splattered, soaked into her skin. Embedded deep beneath her fingernails, caked into her cuticles. There was so much that it looked like dirt, but it wasn't; it was dried blood, thick and dark. It had packed itself so tightly under her nails that it seemed to fuse with her skin, as though she had spent the entire day clawing through the earth, digging her way out of some unearthly grave with her bare hands. In twenty-seven years of law enforcement, the trooper said he had never seen anything like it.

Her hair, once long and beautiful, was now a matted, tangled mess of dried blood. What had once been soft and flowing was transformed into a snarled and knotted mass. The blood had caked her hair into thick, heavy strands, turning it into a hard, dried, gruesome web. And there, buried deep within the blood-soaked tangles, was something that made the trooper's stomach churn. Wait... is that...? It is… a chunk of flesh, wedged like a grotesque secret amidst the tangles of her hair. They pulled it free, yet another piece of evidence from the gruesome scene.

The trooper remembered how, at first glance, Angelee's face seemed strangely tanned, almost healthy in its hue. But as the hospital staff began to wash her, as the warm water soaked into the sponge, the truth was revealed. Beneath the blood, her skin was ghostly white. The blood had covered her so completely that it masked her true complexion, creating the illusion of warmth and life where there was none. The trooper testified that it wasn't normal blood splatter—it was such a fine mist that it had perfectly dried and caked on, like grotesque makeup foundation meticulously applied to hide the horror beneath.

And then, she spoke. Her voice—steady and eerily calm—cut through the room. It was as though she was stating something mundane, a simple fact: "I killed Bill. His soul needed to be cleaned—the dogs told me so."

Those words twisted my reality into something dark, something surreal. I sat there, struggling to process what I had just heard, feeling my world warp around me. This was worse than anything I could have imagined. This wasn't just a nightmare—it was a reckoning, one that would unravel everything I thought I knew about my sister and the world we shared.

This is the story of that nightmare. A story of unimaginable acts, a plunge into a darkness none of us saw coming. Even now, I struggle to make sense of it all, to piece together the fragments left in its wake. But this is where the journey begins—through horror, confusion, and the relentless search for answers in a cruel world that so often offers none.

PART I
WAY BACK WHEN

CHAPTER 1: A DAUGHTER LONG DREAMED OF

Where does mental illness begin? Where does it come from? They say that it's caused by complex combinations of genetic inheritance and environmental factors. Ok, well that seems vague. I've thought about this often over the past couple years, wondering, Where did it start? How? Why? I couldn't figure it out, so my search started at the beginning—the very beginning.

My mom had always held a deep-seated longing for a daughter, a wish that seemed to crystallize long before Angelee was even born. She had carefully chosen the name, inspired by her favorite perfume, Enjoli. She added her own touch of ethereal charm by spelling it as Angelee. It was a name that shimmered with the promise of grace and beauty, as though she believed the name itself would imbue her daughter with the light and warmth that had so often eluded us.

Her hopes extended even further when she gave Angelee the middle name Noel. Christmas was my mom's favorite holiday, and to her, the name Noel carried a deeply angelic meaning. It was as if she wanted to fill Angelee's name with as much joy and hope as possible, crafting it to symbolize all the love and potential she dreamed of for her daughter.

When she found out she was pregnant, her excitement was undeniable. Somehow, she just knew it was going to be a girl—her Angelee. This news brought a rare burst of joy into our lives, lives that were otherwise marked by persistent hardships and struggles. I was seven years old at the time, an age where my understanding was still limited but my enthusiasm was boundless. The thought of having a baby sister was a bright spot that made the heaviness of our daily struggles seem a little lighter. My mom's joy was infectious, and for a brief period, we were all swept up in the promise of something new and hopeful.

I remember the day she told us the news as if it were yesterday, even though it was nearly forty-five years ago. She was practically glowing with excitement. She had chosen a small local diner to mark the occasion, a rare treat in itself since we didn't go out much. Even before she spoke, I knew something special was happening. But when she finally told us she was pregnant, the pure, unfiltered joy on her face was unforgettable. It was the happiest I had ever seen her—perhaps the happiest I would ever see her. Her smile was radiant, and her eyes gleamed with pride. It was as though this baby was the answer to all her prayers, and I felt that joy, too, as though the promise of something better had finally come.

As she spoke, her happiness was contagious. She beamed at everyone who came by our table, sharing the news with anyone who would listen, her excitement spilling out into the diner. I sat there, soaking it in, watching how her eyes sparkled and how excited she was. But as I listened, a question began to form in my mind. Something was missing from this picture, something I had always wondered about, even if I didn't dwell on it too much.

I had seen kids at school with their dads. Some had both parents at home. And here was my mom, happier than I'd ever seen her, but there was no mention of a father. I hesitated, then asked, "What about the baby's dad?"

I don't remember exactly how she responded, but I know she told me he wouldn't be around—no dad. Somehow, that felt normal to me. My own father had left before I turned two, and I had no memory of him. I never knew him, so I never missed him. The news about Angelee's father not being there either just seemed natural to me.

Mom and I had a special song back then—"You and Me Against the World" by Helen Reddy. She'd sing it to me, and every time the line about the monkeys in the circus came up, she'd tap my nose. It was our thing, and I loved those moments. But that night, when we got home, we talked excitedly about Angelee. She told me that while this would always be our song, we'd soon need a new one, one for my sister. I thought it was the neatest thing—we would all have songs!

I was beyond excited. I was the only kid on the block without a sibling, and now I'd finally have one. I couldn't wait to be a big brother—so much so that it made the cramped, chaotic house we lived in seem less important. Even with the constant noise, the animals everywhere, and the rooms that always felt too small, the thought of Angelee coming home filled me with pride and anticipation. I spent hours imagining the things I would teach her and the ways I would protect her, dreaming that this baby might somehow change everything for us.

Of course, reality couldn't be ignored for long. We never had much money, so we lived with Grandma in her house—a modest two-bedroom, one-bath home in Wayne, Michigan. The home, once proud, now showed its wear beneath the relentless weight of age and neglect.

The small, cramped rooms struggled to contain the lives that filled them, each space feeling stretched to its limits.

The animals were part of our everyday life as well. Cats, dogs, and even rabbits seemed to fill every corner, their presence constant. My mom had an unyielding compassion for strays, and while that was admirable, it also added to the chaos of our home. The smell of animals permeated every wall and every carpet. Confined to the basement more often than not, the animals left piles of feces and wet spots as a permanent fixture. The basement itself was a mess—there's just no way to hide this fact. Going down there was always a challenge. I remember tiptoeing through the basement, trying to avoid the worst of it, but it felt like an impossible task. As a kid, I simply went along with it; I hadn't yet learned the importance of keeping things clean.

The thin and tired walls of the house seemed to absorb and echo every argument, every sigh of frustration, and every moment of disappointment. The smell of cigarette smoke and animals was normal. It was as if the house itself was closing in on us, the weight of our struggles pressing against us from all sides. Every groan of the floorboards and every muffled sound from the animals felt like a reminder of the inescapable turmoil that had taken root in our lives Yet, despite everything, this house was home. It was the only home I had ever known.

This now weary house had once been a symbol of pride for my grandparents when they bought it brand new, long before I was born. Back then, it was the first house on the block with a concrete driveway, a detached garage, and central air conditioning—luxuries that set it apart in the neighborhood. A successful businessman, my grandfather had bought a home that was a testament to his achievements and aspirations.

Sadly, I never had the chance to know my grandfather though; he passed away far too soon. The house now stood as a distant echo of a past that felt both cherished and unreachable. Its walls bore silent witness to the years that had worn it down, just as time was now wearing down the lives within it.

When my mom brought Angelee home from the hospital, it felt like a celebration, even in our small, cluttered house. My aunts and cousins gathered in the living room with Grandma and me, all of us waiting eagerly to catch a glimpse of the newest family member. Mom told me to sit on the couch if I wanted to hold her. I climbed up, my legs swinging nervously as I tried to stay as still as possible. When she finally placed Angelee in my arms, she felt so tiny, almost weightless. I remember feeling like I was holding something far too fragile for this world. Her skin was soft, and I watched as her tiny fists peeked out from beneath the blanket she was wrapped in.

I was afraid to move, terrified I might break her or that I wasn't holding her quite right. My heart raced with a mix of excitement and joy, but also fear that I was doing something wrong. And yet, with that fear came an unexpected rush of pride—being a big brother suddenly felt like the most important job in the world. In that moment, all the worry and noise from our everyday lives faded into the background. The room felt lighter, as it was filled with excited chatter and happy whispers. Angelee's arrival shined a light into our lives that hadn't been there before, and I was so happy.

Angelee's arrival was marked by her full head of blonde curls and striking blue eyes—a dazzling contrast to the drab reality of our living conditions. She truly was everything my mom had dreamed of, a living embodiment of her hopes and dreams. But the reality of our small house quickly tempered the initial euphoria. The addition of a new family member soon made our already cramped living space feel even smaller. Mom made some significant adjustments, converting the upstairs loft into a makeshift nursery and her own new bedroom. This move gave me my own first-floor bedroom right next to Grandma's. However, what was meant to be a positive change was quickly overshadowed by the necessity of squeezing every single inch out of our home for practicality.

I can still picture the narrow hallway door that led up to the attic loft and its long, narrow staircase that turned sharply to the right at the top. Those stairs felt like a barrier that separated our cramped reality from the small zone of comfort Mom was trying to create for Angelee. Her crib was nestled on a small landing at the top of the stairs, and beyond it, the loft opened into the bedroom Mom had painstakingly created.

The nursery, while a testament to Mom's resourcefulness, was also a constant reminder of how our dreams and reality often collided. The upstairs, with its makeshift partitions and repurposed furniture, stood as a tangible symbol of the compromise between hope and practicality that defined our lives in that house.

CHAPTER 2: CHAOS BENEATH THE SURFACE

Our family dynamic was a constant source of instability. Our home was always crowded, with a quiet unease when we got along and a heavy tension when conflict took over. We lived in a constant state of precarious balance, often threatened by the weight of our circumstances.

During those storms, when our ship was lost at sea and the waves were crashing upon us, Grandma was the needle on the compass that kept us pointed north. The pressure of everything always seemed to fall heavily on her shoulders, and she did her best to keep things held together. She was a soft-spoken woman of quiet strength, and though she was older, she was determined—a scholar of practiced patience. Every step she took was marked by the effort of maintaining some semblance of normalcy in our lives.

Sundays were sacred to her. Church was her sanctuary; it was the one place where she could momentarily recenter herself and find balance. Whether I liked it or not, Sunday mornings were always spent with her, unless I could convincingly pretend to oversleep. Sunday morning church wasn't just a routine; it was an obligation. I believe this was where she found her strength, the lifeline she clung to when everything else felt like it was unraveling.

Angelee went with us too, even as a baby. She would be all dressed up in her Sunday best. Grandma took great care in picking each dress out for her. When the church bus pulled up in front of the house, I had Angelee in one arm and hooked Grandma's arm with the other, helping her out to the bus and up those janky, rubber-covered stairs. I think it was an old school bus in its prior life. I have to admit, the bus rides were actually kind of fun. There were a lot of other kids that rode it too. I was generally tasked with keeping an eye on Angelee during church, unless she went to the nursery, but that wasn't often.

Grandma, ever proud and proper, did her best to uphold appearances during service. She loved it; she had so many friends there. She did a great job of presenting a polished front to them, and the congregation loved her just as much. But even then, I could see the strain in her. There was something unspoken in the way she moved. She carried herself with a quiet dignity, despite the weight of home bearing down on her.

There were moments when sitting in those old, long, wooden pews that I'd glance over at her and see strength in her eyes. That unwavering determination to keep our little world from collapsing. She was the glue that held us together when Mom wasn't around—which was often. And even though I didn't, or couldn't, see it at the time, I now realize Grandma wasn't just holding us together for the sake of survival; she was trying to give us a sense of stability, something solid and unshakable. Because we lived in a world where it felt like the ground was constantly shifting beneath our feet.

Our mom worked long hours and was gone most mornings before I even woke up. It was Grandma who made sure I was up for school on time, even when I fought her every step of the way. She made sure I grabbed something to eat before heading out to school. She took care of Angelee as a baby and then as a toddler. Looking back, I can't imagine how hard it must have been on her, taking care of two kids while juggling everything else. But back then, it was just life; I didn't know any other way.

Our house was also a revolving door for people who needed a place to stay. Mostly, it was different cousins or uncles, but sometimes it was Mom's friends. They usually stayed on the couch, but those who stayed longer would often move into the basement and try to make it livable. I remember feeling a strange mix of emotions the first few times it happened. On one hand, I felt relieved that the long-neglected basement was finally being cleaned. On the other hand, I felt horrible for them having to live down in the damp basement with that stench. It wasn't a place to live comfortably, but I guess if you needed a place badly enough, you made do.

Mom's friends and family weren't the only ones who passed through; one time, it was her boyfriend. It was my eleventh birthday when he moved in. The memory of that day is one I'll never forget. It was supposed to be a special day, starting out with just Angelee, me, and our Saturday morning cartoons.

Back then, Saturday morning cartoons were a ritual. It was the only time you could binge-watch cartoons for hours. As a baby, she would be mesmerized by anything I had on. When she became a toddler, we started alternating shows—she'd get to pick for half an hour, then I'd pick for the next. It didn't really matter because we loved them all. Except for that one show about some magic pony. I think she picked it just because I hated it.

I remember one Saturday, we were sitting in the middle of the floor, and it was time for that pony show. I thought I'd be clever. I stood up, walked over to our large, floor-model TV, and, well, back then, TVs had manual dials. You had to physically turn the dial to change the channel to one of the three or four we had. I pretended like I was going to change the channel and then pulled the dial off the front of the TV. The dial was actually removable, but to a little girl, it looked like I'd broken it and she thought the channel couldn't be changed. For a moment, I felt like a genius. I'd figured out how to keep the channel on my superhero show instead of the pony show. Of course, Angelee cried, and Mom came in and made me put the dial back on. The pony show won in the end, but for that moment, I felt like I had scored a genius badge straight out of a comic strip.

This particular birthday morning, though, things went south quickly. We were watching cartoons—maybe Scooby-Doo or The Smurfs, I'm not sure why those stick in my mind—when Mom walked in. She said something, but I don't remember the exact words. I do remember the sheer excitement in her voice as she spoke. When we turned away from the TV to look at her, that's when we saw him. A tall, burly man stood awkwardly next to her. She introduced him as her boyfriend and casually mentioned he was moving in with us, oh, and that he had just gotten out of prison.

My heart sank. It was supposed to be my special day. My birthday. Mom looked so excited, and he just stood there, emotionless. Then he did it—that half-jerk smile of his. One side of his mouth curled up in the most non-genuine smile. And he spoke in what felt like the most ridiculous, fake country accent, "Hey y'all." I stood up, muttered "hi," and went straight to my room. I was furious.

We didn't know she had a boyfriend, let alone someone who had just been released from prison. The excitement of the day vanished. So much for our carefree Saturday morning; it had turned into something darker. I stayed in my room most of the day, only coming out when my aunts and cousins arrived for my birthday party later that afternoon.

Looking back, I realize how tense the atmosphere was that day. No one seemed to know this guy or that he would be moving in. He was a stranger in our home. I felt like my birthday had been stolen, completely overshadowed by his presence. For the first time, I heard prison stories. He told them with such enthusiasm in front of everyone, like they made him sound cool or worldly. But the truth was, those stories scared us all.

Not long after he moved in, things got worse. One day, Angelee and I were playing in the living room when we heard Mom scream from upstairs. It was a sound I had never heard before. It was raw and filled with terror, and it pierced through the entire house. Without thinking, I flew up those narrow stairs, my heart pounding as if it was going to burst right out of my chest. When I reached the top and rounded the corner, I froze. It was like a nightmare. He was on top of Mom, who was lying on the bed. His fist was raised high in the air and then he brought it down fast and hard on her head.

Tears streaming down my face, my voice shaking, I screamed at him to stop. He whipped his head toward me, snarling, "Get out!" I had never heard such true anger in someone's voice. I panicked, grabbed the first thing I saw—my Trapper Keeper notebook—and threw it at him as hard as I could. It bounced off him harmlessly but distracted him from Mom long enough for him to lunge toward me. I took off running down the stairs and straight through the living room, headed for the front door. Angelee was still in the living room when I ran past, her body trembling, her face red with tears. She looked at me with pleading eyes, begging me for help. But I couldn't stop, I was too afraid. I ran straight to my best friend's house down the street, bursting through the door without knocking.

Between sobs and wiping tears from my face, I told my friend's mom what had happened. She called the police, and we stood outside, watching from a distance as they arrived. They handcuffed him and took him away in the back of their squad car. There were no sirens, just the flashing lights illuminating everything in bursts of red and blue. It was the last time we ever saw him.

When I finally returned home, the house was quiet. Mom was sitting on the couch, clutching a still-terrified Angelee tightly, both of them crying. The trauma of that day lingered long after the incident. For days, Angelee would wake up in the middle of the night, screaming, or sobbing uncontrollably. She hadn't seen the violence herself, but the fear had left its mark. The scars from the event were etched into her memory. No matter how hard I tried to protect her, I couldn't shield her from the chaos that seemed to follow us.

Despite the hardships, there were glimmers of light that broke through the darkness. Those moments of reprieve, however fleeting, became our lifelines. We would find solace in laughter, and in those shared bursts of joy, the weight of our struggles seemed to lift, if only for a while. Angelee was often at the heart of these moments. Her laughter—loud, vivid, hearty, and full of life—had a way of piercing through the gloom that clung to us, bringing warmth and connection to our small world. Even in the midst of mayhem, we found ways to create joy, to cling to the threads of happiness that held us together.

Mom's exhaustion was a constant, visible strain. Her weariness manifested in her every gesture. The burden of providing for us often led to outbursts of frustration, making the warm, loving family moments you see on television seem like a distant dream. Instead, we learned to navigate around each other, each of us walking on eggshells, careful not to add to the ever-present stress that surrounded us.

As time went on, the fissures in our family dynamic grew deeper. There was an eight-year gap between Angelee and me that created a chasm that was hard to bridge. I resented the attention she demanded, but I also felt a deep responsibility to protect her. The truth was, I was still just a kid myself. I was trying to cope with and understand a world that always seemed indifferent to our struggles.

Angelee never sought to be a burden; she simply longed to be included, to be part of the action, and to feel loved. Her energy was boundless. She was hyper and impulsive, always in motion, and always eager to engage. She would often burst into my room, her eyes alight with anticipation as she tried to drag me into her imaginative play. Her favorite pastime was playing with her Cabbage Patch dolls, and she was relentless in her efforts to involve me in her make-believe world.

When I refused—as I often did, preferring my own solitary pursuits—her disappointment would swiftly transform into anger. Her temper could flare up unpredictably, and she would storm off in frustration. Though I felt a pang of guilt seeing her upset, I rationalized it to myself with the thought, That's just not what boys do.

On the occasions when I did engage with her, Angelee's reaction was nothing short of jubilant. Her face would light up with unrestrained joy, as if my willingness to spend time with her was the greatest gift. I could never quite predict her response to my moods or decisions, but one thing was clear: when she was happy, her enthusiasm was infectious and uplifting. Conversely, when she was upset, her emotions dominated the room, creating an undeniable shift in the atmosphere that affected everyone around her.

Reflecting on those early years, it's evident that our childhood was far from the idyllic vision one might hope for. We had just enough to survive but little beyond that. Mom did her best, but the strain of our circumstances was irrefutable. As I grew older, I began to grasp the fragility of our situation more acutely. Life was a series of challenges, and the harsh reality was that it would only grow more difficult as time went on.

CHAPTER 3:
CAGED IN THE SHACK

Our life in Wayne had always been difficult, but it became even worse when we moved across Michigan Avenue to a place called "Shack Town." I don't remember the exact reason we had to move from Grandma's house, I only knew it wasn't because we chose to.

The new neighborhood was a whole new world with a whole new feel. You could tell it was a much poorer area than where Grandma lived. The homes were neglected. Grass or weeds grew tall in so many yards, and everything was just more worn down and hopeless looking. The neighborhood was lined with aging duplexes and a few single-story homes. They were built during the 1940s to accommodate the military personnel and workers from the nearby defense industry plants. At the time, resources were scarce, so they were constructed with whatever materials were available. Most of the homes even lacked gutters. After the war, these homes were sold to the public, and most of them became low-income rental homes.

Our new home on Shiawassee Court was a tiny, single-story house at the end of the cul-de-sac. I thought Grandma's house was small, but this thing, it was tiny. Both were two-bedroom, one-bathroom homes, but at least at Grandma's you had an upstairs and a basement. There you could kind of find somewhere to get away, to try to breathe. Not here, though.

The inside of this house had floors that sagged in spots. They didn't go through to the crawl space, they just literally sagged beneath your feet as you walked. There were also some really cool designs from water damage on the ceilings where the roof leaked from too many Michigan winters. And then there were the walls. They were so thin that you could hear every fight outside and every police or fire truck siren wailing through the streets, which was rather constant there.

The house itself was dark and cramped, as if shadows hung around just a bit longer than they should have. Despite its shortcomings, though, Mom was super proud of it. It was her first real house. She did her very best to create some sense of stability by making it our home.

The day we moved in, her boyfriend moved in too. They had been seeing each other for a little while at this point. With him moving in, it seemed as if he was there to stay. He was big, muscular and intimidating. I hadn't ever encountered anyone quite like him before. He was pretty scary, both in his appearance and how he acted. Just the way he looked at you and the way he said your name in that harsh, deep tone was enough to freeze you in your tracks.

He worked day jobs here and there in construction, but his real job was selling drugs. People either respected him or feared him, and it was hard to tell which was which. For Angelee and me, we just knew he was a guy who didn't really like kids much, so he was someone to avoid, which was difficult in our small house.

The house was impossibly small for the four of us. There wasn't enough room to really move around, let alone live comfortably. My room was little more than a large closet by the front door that shared space with the water heater and washing machine. There wasn't even room for a dryer, so we didn't have one. Clothes drying was done outside on the clothesline during the nice weather and the laundromat during bad weather.

Angelee's room wasn't much better, though she did have four walls with a door. She spent most of her time in there playing—or hiding, whatever you want to call it. At five years old, Angelee already knew how to tiptoe around the adults in the house. She'd tell me about how she tried to stay in her room all day, scared of doing something that might piss Mom or her boyfriend off. The times when I was home, which wasn't often, she'd sneak out to the kitchen and steal a snack or come into my room and just hang out. Anyone could have seen the fear in her eyes. The angst she felt was obvious even if she never talked about it.

I was spending more and more time away from home those days. I'd go anywhere just to escape for a while. Playing outside, going to a friend's house, the arcade, or the woods to play. Anywhere that felt less oppressive. I always felt guilty leaving her there, but I was still struggling internally and trying to manage the only way I knew how.

Angelee was just like Mom—she had a bleeding heart for animals. I still to this day think they were her only real, true comfort during those years. It all started with a cat she found and brought home. She named him Heathcliff, after the cartoon character. He quickly became a part of our family, and he fit in with our two dogs, Snowball and Bull. Both of those dogs were mixed breeds, or "mutts" as Mom called them, that we got from somewhere I can't remember. They were mostly housebroken, but they had a real knack for causing destruction.

One day, we came home from picking up our monthly government food allotment—they called it Focus Hope—and the dogs were in the kitchen, running back and forth. We were all surprised because normally, Mom's boyfriend locked them in that small bathroom whenever we left, because they destroyed stuff. Not today, though. Today, they had clearly had the run of the house for quite some time. It wasn't until we saw the bathroom door that we realized how they'd gotten out. They clawed and chewed their way through the door! Mom and her boyfriend were pissed! Despite my shock, I looked on in amazement, marveling at their determination. I remember silently chuckling because I couldn't really blame them, there were many days when I would have done the exact same thing to escape.

Angelee's endless compassion meant she always kept some animal food in her pockets when she went out to play. She knew she would encounter some strays, and she wanted to feed them, to give them something she knew was scarce in this world—a full belly, a moment of care, a bit of warmth. I loved this about her. In a world that surely felt cold and unkind to her, Angelee's kindness towards these animals was a rare and beautiful thing.

There was a point in time where I had worked up the nerve to make my escape, to run away from home. I'd always had the desire, but never the nerve. This day was different; Mom was gone to work and her boyfriend was working a construction job—it was the perfect opportunity. Angelee was at Grandma's house. I packed up my duffle bag, grabbed my BB gun, and made my escape. I thought for sure one of the neighbors would see me and call Mom, but no one stopped me or seemed to care… or so I thought.

I remember the rush of fear and adrenaline as I ran down the street. I'm sure I looked foolish as I ducked behind trees and cars trying not to be seen. Then I reached the woods and the feeling of dread started to subside. The woods were my safe space, allowing me to feel as though I was able to hide without ever being found. I walked through the trees all the way to the other end of the forest, right to the tree line.

A large field between me and the road was where I sat. With my back up against a tree, I stared at the cars going by. I sat there for hours lost in my thoughts. I tried to imagine the lives of the people inside each vehicle, the places they were headed. I wondered if any of them had ever felt as lost and aimless as I did in that moment.

Eventually, I knew I had to go. Where? I didn't know, but something was telling me it was time to start moving, to go as fast and far as I could. Fate seemed to have other plans. Just as I'd started to stand, Mom's boyfriend came barreling down the road in his dump truck. Pure fear shot through me as he slammed his truck to the shoulder of the road and jumped out. Startled and shocked, I bolted. I dropped everything and ran. I ran as fast as I could, my heart pounding in my ears. I ran across the street to the nearby houses and started climbing and jumping over fences in people's backyards. But he was relentless, his heavy boots hitting the ground with the same force as my fear. He was hurdling those exact same fences, somehow not even touching them as he went over each of them. I remember thinking, How is this even possible?

When he finally caught up to me, he was laughing; to this day I still wonder why. I felt his grip on my arm, like a vice locking me in place. He dragged me back to his truck and threw me inside. We drove straight back to Shiawassee Court.

When we pulled up in front of the house, I saw Mom and Angelee standing in the front yard. It was over, I was caught and dragged back home. As I reached for the door handle to let myself out, he yanked me back with such a force that it stunned me. In one swift motion, he threw me across the front seat and out the driver's door, sending me crashing into the pavement so hard I bounced. The pain was unforgettable, shooting through me like lightning, but what I remember the most was looking up and seeing Angelee's face. Her little face was bright red, tears flowing down her cheeks. That look still haunts me. Her eyes were wide and filled with a raw, unfiltered terror that it makes my chest tighten even right now. She had never encountered such violence before. Seeing her like that and knowing she had been exposed to this shattered something deep inside me.

I was grounded, of course. Confined to my tiny closet room. For three days, Angelee never left my side. She stayed with me, refusing to leave. She never asked me much, just simple questions like, "Why did you leave? Where were you going? Why didn't you take me with you?" I didn't have any answers for her, though. I felt as if I had failed her. It was times like this when the eight-year gap didn't even seem to exist. We were always there to comfort each other in the darkest times.

CHAPTER 4:
A FATHER RETURNS

As life went on, Angelee's behavior started to shift in ways nobody expected, even though we probably should have. The sweet, playful little girl who loved her Cabbage Patch dolls began to slowly change, revealing a mixture of unpredictability and defiance. It was as if she was pushing back against the heavy burden life had placed on her far too early. At such a young age, she was beginning to understand that life didn't always make sense, and was seldom fair. That when things went wrong, there wasn't always someone around to make them right.

But then, seemingly out of nowhere, her father appeared in her life.

I think it was sometime during the spring when we got to meet Angelee's father; it was the first time either of us had ever met him. He was nice. I recall thinking he was a "cool country dude." He was married and lived about thirty minutes away in a prominent, small town. I don't remember exactly what brought him to her, but from my understanding, his heart had been yearning to meet Angelee, and he desired to get to know his daughter. I don't think the reason mattered to her. It was new and exciting, a shift in the routine we'd grown so used to.

His house had a real backyard with actual green grass that was kept nicely mowed. It had big, beautiful flower gardens that lined the property, and it even had a real deal white picket fence. The place looked like it came straight out of a movie set; it was absolutely gorgeous. Angelee was thrilled at the idea of going to stay with him on the weekends, and it felt like things might finally be turning around for her.

That first weekend she went over there, I remember it well. She left with a mixture of nervousness and quiet excitement. It was a totally new experience, and I could tell she clearly didn't know what to expect. They threw her a party—an honest-to-god party!—and cooked so much food on the grill. She got to meet so many new relatives from his side, people who welcomed her with open arms. They were kind, enthusiastic and genuinely thrilled to meet her. For the first time since she was brought home from the hospital as a baby, she was the star, the center of attention. Everyone gathered to meet her, and she absolutely loved it.

When she came back from that first weekend at her dad's house, she was practically glowing! There was a lightness in her step, a kind of joy and happiness I hadn't seen in a long time. As if the usual weight she had to carry around had been lifted, even if only temporary. She spoke with so much excitement about everything, like the huge, soft bed she got to sleep in and how his wife had baked cookies just for her! There was so much warmth and laughter that had filled the house. It was such a stark contrast to the tension and chaos of our house. I could see just how much that visit meant to her, and how excited she was to go back. It gave her a glimpse of something different, something better.

Well, seeing how much fun she was having, it didn't take long before I asked if I could go too. I wasn't quite sure how her dad would feel about it; after all, I wasn't his kid. When Angelee asked him, he was quick to respond that he didn't mind. It was, in fact, almost as if he was relieved to have me there. Like me being there somehow helped take some of the pressure off of him. So I went, sometimes more and sometimes less, but enough to feel as if I was able to have my own brief escape as well.

Being over there felt like stepping into a different world. The contrast was so brilliant it was almost disorientating. Their fridge was always full of food, the beds were so soft and comfortable, and everything was so clean that, to us, it was unnatural. We finally found a place that made those TV shows feel not quite as impossible as they once seemed. For a couple of days every other week, Angelee could finally breathe. She was free from the tension, the fighting, and the mayhem that clung to our everyday lives at home. It was so easy to see it in Angelee; she seemed to walk taller, and she came home relaxed and excited. For the first time in a long time, the anxiety of walking on eggshells at home had faded for both of us—even if only for a while.

Angelee loved when they would buy her clothes; she got clothes that still had the original price tags on them. The outfits made her light up with excitement. They would take her to get her hair done, which made her feel as if she mattered. And his wife was so kind and warm. She would let her help with cooking meals, because almost every meal there was actually homemade. I remember watching Angelee smile and laugh as she learned, her eyes wide with fascination. She'd carry on about what she was learning, talking all about ingredients and recipes, completely immersed in being a kid. It was fun to watch, but more than that, it was a relief. For once, she wasn't scared or weighed down with uncertainty. She was just a little girl having fun.

And for quite some time, things seemed so much better. Angelee was happier on those weekends, and I was more than grateful for the breaks when I got to go as well. But hell, deep down, I knew it couldn't last forever. Nothing good ever lasted long in our lives, and sure enough, after a while, it all came crashing down.

CHAPTER 5: SHATTERED ROOTS

We knew there had been some tension at her dad's house for a while at this point, though it was very different from the kind of tension we were used to. Angelee and I were both very versed in reading and detecting the signs, watching for the small unspoken cues that hinted at unease. She would occasionally make passing comments to me about arguments she had overheard outside, at the dinner table, or upstairs. They were usually made with hushed tones that the adults probably didn't think she would, or could, understand. But she picked up on them, just like we always did at home. It wasn't really the same loud, crazy arguing we lived with, but it was still there nonetheless. It was a quieter, subtler uncomfortableness that you could sense in the air.

The day things changed, we were at home when her dad called. Mom answered the phone and gave it to Angelee. She grabbed the phone with a huge smile and ran off to her room, shutting the door softly behind her. She was in there for what felt like forever, but when she did finally come out, something about her had shifted. Her face was pale, her eyes swollen and red from crying. She didn't really need to say anything for me to know that whatever had been said wasn't good news.

I thought maybe he just cancelled on her for that weekend; it didn't happen often, but it had happened before. When Angelee finally did speak, her words were filled with sorrow. Her dad had told her that he and his wife were getting a divorce, and when he got settled again, they could restart their visits. Just like that, it was over. Her escape, the one place where she felt free from the weight of the world, had vanished in that instant. The safety net she had been clinging to had been ripped away, and all that was left was the comfort of chaos at home.

The loss of those weekends hit Angelee harder than I had imagined. She'd had a taste of what life could be like—what it should have been like—and now, it was gone. I don't think it was really just the comfort of a clean house, the warm meals, or the new clothes that she missed. It was the feeling of being seen, of being cared about and for, and having a place where she could enjoy her youth. Her little world had shattered again, and she was clearly unsure of how to put it back together. It was the last time we saw him for a very, very long time.

The changes in her were immediately noticeable. It wasn't that she was just sad, she was downright mad. That lightness she was showing was gone, replaced with a brooding cloud of silence. She became quieter, more withdrawn, and started showing an edge. Resentment simmered beneath the surface. It deeply hardened her in a new way, and that heaviness was right back on those tiny little shoulders of hers. I couldn't blame her for being mad.

Our life was back in full force of the unpredictability, but this time, there were no escapes. No weekend sanctuary to break up the monotony of our frenzied lives. Without that reprieve, it felt like the walls were back to closing in on her, and I didn't know how to help.

With that fleeting sense of stability gone, things at home were right back to the way they had always been. Same old weekends, same old routines, same old fighting. We did get to start a new pattern, though it really wasn't all that fun. We started moving, drifting from one run-down house to another. Each place seemed more temporary than the last, but the houses and the neighborhoods all stayed the same, and the chaos always found us. It was as if we were living in a constant state of upheaval; we could never stay anywhere long enough to feel settled or secure. Every move hit the reset button on our lives. Yet, nothing ever really changed.

Angelee never had any trouble making new friends wherever we landed. Her outgoing nature always drew people to her. The trouble was she could never keep them. As soon as she would start creating a new bond with someone, we'd pack up and leave. Sometimes, we would have a little warning, sometimes we didn't have any. One day Angelee would be laughing it up and playing with her new best friend, and the next, we'd be loading everything up, leaving another home and another friendship behind. The instability would gnaw at her, chipping away at the foundation of the person she was trying to become. She just couldn't understand the frustrations. Every time we started putting down roots, life ripped them out, leaving her to start over again in unfamiliar soil.

I tried to cope in my own ways. I'd bury myself in my video games and stay out of the house as much as possible. The less time I spent at home, the easier it was to deal with everything. Angelee wasn't like me. She longed for connection, stability, for something solid that she could hold onto. She craved the kind of relationships that made her feel grounded, as if she truly belonged somewhere. And with every move, every lost friend, that dream seemed to slip further and further out of her reach. Each time we packed up and left, she lost another piece of the foundation she was trying so hard to build, and it was taking a noticeable toll on her.

CHAPTER 6: A STAGE FULL OF DREAMS

There was one house we moved into that was one of the nicest rentals we lived in. In this house, we all had our very own bedrooms, and on top of that, Angelee and I shared our own bathroom. We were living the high life! For the first time, we had hopes that things were starting to look up. The walls weren't caving in, the floors were strong and straight, and best of all, there was room to breathe.

Despite the relative calm, something was brewing.

I was walking by Angelee's room one day not long after we had moved in. I saw her sitting there, staring blankly at the floor as I passed by. Her beloved dolls, and many other things, were scattered around the room, almost as if forgotten. It was strange seeing Angelee's room like this. Normally, she always kept her things neat and tidy, as she was almost obsessive about protecting them. As if they were the only things she could control in a life that defied all attempts at control. The disarray revealed something was simmering deep beneath the surface.

Her room was rather large, but that day it felt stifling. The air was thick, and the quiet had a way of pressing down on me as I entered. The force of it was there, those unsaid words, the emotions neither of us really knew how to express. Angelee sat there, quiet and still, her curly hair falling messily over her face. She never once bothered to push it aside. There was almost a lifelessness about her that was so different from the girl who could light up any room with her energy and laughter.

I was unsure of what to say, but I still sat down beside her. The dull light from the window cast long shadows that made the room feel much smaller than it was. For a while it felt as if time had stopped as we sat there in silence. The sound from the TV in the living room, the general hum of the house, the usual background noises of the world all faded into the distance.

Finally, Angelee spoke, her voice barely more than a whisper. "Why does everything keep changing?"

Her words cut through the silence. They were simple, yet loaded with the kind of heartbreak no kid should have to bear. She didn't even look at me when she asked it. Her eyes stayed fixed on the floor, as if the answer might be hidden in the clutter that surrounded her. I knew what she was really asking. Why did we keep moving? Why couldn't we stay in one place long enough to feel secure? Why did her brief glimpses of happiness, like the weekends with her dad, always slip away? Why is mom never around? Why does everyone always fight? What did I do to deserve all of this?

I didn't have an answer for her. I didn't have any answers for her. I wish I had. I wanted to tell her things would get better, that stability was just around the corner. But the truth was, I didn't know. All I knew was that it was getting harder and harder to keep up acting like things were fine, that things would get better one day. The uncertainty of our lives loomed over us like a dark cloud that never really went away.

The room felt even quieter after that. I could hear her breathing, soft and steady. It was clear the weight of the world was still being carried by her small shoulders. I hated it. I hated seeing her like this. So lost, so burdened. I didn't know how to help her, so most of the time, I couldn't.

We stayed there in that suffocating silence for what seemed like forever. Neither of us knew what to do with the sadness that hung between us. I wanted to reach out, to tell her that we'd get through it somehow, but the words never came. All I could do was sit beside her, hoping that maybe, just maybe, being there was enough.

In the midst of everything, something amazing happened: she made a new friend. These two clicked instantly. They were both in the same grade and were overloaded with energy and full of dreams. They were inseparable. Every free minute they had, they spent it together. It didn't matter if it was over at our house or hers, they were always side by side giggling or planning their next big adventure. That friendship was everything to Angelee, and it came at the most perfect time.

It was the announcement of their school's talent show, that's when their closeness went to a whole new level. It was the biggest event in both of their lives. She and her friend decided that they would not only enter and perform, but they were absolutely convinced that they would win the whole thing. Their excitement was infectious. They practiced every day, jumping and dancing around the living room, blaring the song they were going to use. I remember the giggling was nonstop, and although I hate to admit it, I'm smiling as I say their laughter was almost annoying at times. Angelee spoke about the performance with every breath she took. Busting into the room, bouncing with giddiness. Her face was always lit up as she spoke of their detailed routine, their costumes, and exactly how they were going to dazzle everyone. She was so happy, so full of life.

I can still see them in the living room practicing with their homemade microphones. They had taken empty toilet paper rolls, glued a big Styrofoam ball to one end, then painted them and covered the tops with glitter. These were not just props, they were symbols of how much they believed in their performance. They wore those super-cool outfits that looked like a mash-up of Rainbow Brite and Punky Brewster. There were so many colors and mismatched accessories. It was hilarious, a real sight to see for sure. The 'old' Angelee was not only back, but back and full of life!

When the night of the talent show finally arrived, the school gym was packed with people—parents, children, school staff. The atmosphere was buzzing with excitement. It smelled like popcorn and sweat in there, but that's typical of all school gym events, I guess. Kids were running around, laughing and horse playing. It was so loud with the way the voices bounced around everywhere. The lights were bright, harsh almost, glaring down onto that stage. You could see the kids all dressed up and ready to perform. I remember feeling the nervous tension, the thrill of all the little moments leading up to their big performance.

Mom was there that night. We sat together with one of her friends who was able to come along. We were all joking around, it was so much fun.

I watched Angelee and her friend take the stage. Their eyes were wide and bright as they stood there waiting to begin. They really did have the coolest outfits that night. The song began blasting through the stage speakers—Bon Jovi's "Livin' on a Prayer"—and there they went, lip syncing their hearts out and dancing around. It didn't matter that they weren't perfect. They bounced around with infectious enthusiasm, their glittery, homemade microphones in their hands, just shining like the stars they believed they were.

Of course, they didn't win. But that didn't really seem to matter too much to them. They were glowing, had had the time of their lives, and were convinced that they had nailed it. They came up with a theory after the show. They believed they hadn't won because the kid that did, well, his mom worked at the school. It became this whole big conspiracy thing in their minds, a source of endless speculation and something to laugh at.

It was easy to see just how much this companionship meant to Angelee, and I'm so grateful that she had her as a friend. Losing this one, when the time eventually came, would be the hardest loss I ever saw her go through.

CHAPTER 7: GOING FULL CIRCLE

One evening, Mom's boyfriend was arrested. For what, I'll probably never know. But he was out of the picture, and that was when we found out we were losing our house, again. She couldn't keep paying the rent on time, or at all for that matter. Whatever the reason, it didn't make a difference in the end. We packed up in the middle of the night and left. This time, we went back to Grandma's house. I was relieved.

Going back to Grandma's felt strange, but Angelee and I were both super excited. The house seemed much larger that I remembered, and I'm sure it felt even bigger to Angelee. In reality, though, it was still the same house. The two bedrooms on the first floor were still the same, and Grandma still had one of them as hers. Mom quickly started moving her things into the other first-floor bedroom. Angelee was lucky enough to be able to stake claim and move her room to the one upstairs; at this point, it had mostly been finished out. Someone had put paneling on the walls and laid down vinyl flooring, probably to make it easier to clean up after the animals that were running freely throughout the house. It wasn't perfect by any means, but it was hers and she was happy.

As for me, well, I was relegated to the basement. Yes, that same basement where the dogs were allowed to do their business. That mess was impossible to clean, but I was older now, and the idea of having my own space, even down there, was something I could accept.

We made do, as we always did. We cleaned and cleaned, and when that wasn't quite enough, we cleaned some more. The grit and grime had clearly taken root in the house over the years, so cleaning was a never-ending task. Although, there was something about being back that felt familiar, normal even. It wasn't exactly comforting, but it was stable in a way our last number of years had never been.

Sure enough, it wasn't long before Mom had a new boyfriend that moved in. He was always around, just hovering in the background. Unlike the men who had come before him, he wasn't necessarily mean, though. He was kind to Angelee. He didn't really yell and he didn't work, but it wasn't overwhelming having him there.

I was in high school and was gone every waking moment at this point. Every second of freedom I could find, I took it. Nobody seemed to care too much that I wasn't around. Though it wasn't just me who was rarely home; Mom was always gone, too. Mom was actually gone more than ever, often disappearing for days at a time with her boyfriend or working, leaving everyone to fend for themselves.

Grandma was now much older and more frail, so she was finding it harder to move around the house. She was once the rock that held everything together, but now, even getting up the stairs was impossible. Her energy, once full of vigor, had waned, and it left her dependent on the rest of us.

There was another change that happened while we were gone. The animals multiplied—a lot. What had started with good intentions of some rescues and strays that were brought home years ago had spiraled into something nobody was able to manage. Those cats were the worst. They bred unimaginably fast and were everywhere. They lurked under beds, in closets and even in the attic. They'd disappear into the heat ducts somehow and remain hidden for long periods of time. They weren't even able to be counted it was so bad. Quite a few of them were feral, specifically mean and fearful of humans. All of them were living in the same house. A house that had become more theirs than ours.

This, of course, meant that the smell was another problem altogether. It wasn't just the familiar scent of pets, it was that overwhelming, pungent odor of cat urine. It soaked into everything. There was no getting rid of it, let alone even trying to hide it. No matter how much we cleaned or how many air fresheners were put out, that acrid ammonia scent clung to everything. Including the clothes Angelee and I would wear to school. We tried to laugh it off to our peers saying things like, "That's just what happens when you have a zoo at home," or, "Well, when you spend your time rescuing animals, this is what happens." But the truth was, it embarrassed us horribly, and the kids at school never let us forget it.

Angelee loved the animals, all of them. She found a certain level of comfort in them, especially for the ones that allowed her to cuddle with them. They appeared to fill some sort of void she had. Maybe they were something soft and reliable in a house full of uncertainty. But, as more animals appeared—either being brought home or by multiplying—even she started to become overwhelmed. It really was too much for anyone to handle. The constant noise and the endless cleaning was absolutely exhausting, even with her unwavering love of animals. At such a young age, she was growing tired of the turmoil. Yet, she was trapped just like the rest of us.

There was a point when most of the family stopped visiting; it really was just too much for anyone. The overwhelming smell coupled with all the dog and cat hair that covered everything made it hard for anyone to stay very long. It caused quite the rift with our extended family. We learned how much it sucked having to navigate so much family drama.

There were times when we—well, Angelee mostly—were given the task of rounding up and capturing as many kittens as possible. She would then take them to Kmart to try and find them new homes. So, catching those cats and kittens was a spectator sport straight out of those Saturday morning cartoons. Some of them were so untamed and scared of people that we had to come up with some rather ingenious tricks in order to even catch them.

As Angelee chased these cats, I watched in a mixture of awe and amusement. There were times when we resorted to real live traps my uncle had brought over. It wasn't much fun back then, but looking back now, it was hilarious.

In the Kmart parking lot, Angelee would just sit there, either at the end of the parking lot or right up front by the front doors. It wasn't a glamorous job, but there she was, trying her hardest to find these kittens a loving home. There was something so sweet about her quiet determination to find those animals a better life, even if it meant she would have to sit through the heat or cold. She would wait patiently, committed to finding the right people to come along.

With Mom gone all the time and Grandma growing older, Angelee started stepping into the role no child should have to fill. She started to become Grandma's caretaker, and the caretaker of the house as well.

She embraced it at first. She had always been such a caring soul, so stepping up to help Grandma just seemed so natural to her. Over time, those lines started to blur, and what began as a natural kindness started to feel like a daily obligation.

With no one else around to help with anything, Angelee quietly started taking on more and more responsibility. Outwardly, it didn't look like she resented it, at least not yet.

I saw the change in her demeanor, though. She held a quiet acceptance within, a maturity that she shouldn't have had at that age. It was starting to become clear that taking care of Grandma, dealing with all the animals, and just surviving in that house was weighing her down. I never heard her complain about it, though. She was instinctively nurturing and had a sense of duty from within.

As for me, I was just trying to finish up high school, to cross the finish line so I could move out. I was spending even more time away from home, seeking any distraction and trying to find myself. I had one goal in mind: escape. The day after I graduated, I left without looking back. I was determined to start a new life far away from the chaos and instability I had grown up in.

I did know that leaving meant abandoning Angelee, and I felt terrible about that. She was only ten years old when I left, leaving her to face it all alone. I tried to justify it by telling myself that maybe things would get easier for her without me around. Maybe, just maybe, without me there, the tension in the house would ease up a little bit for her. I had to believe that even though deep down, I knew it wasn't true. That guilt sat like a heavy stone in my gut for a long time, but my need to escape was stronger.

As life started moving forward for me so many miles away, I didn't think about Angelee's struggles very often. It's not something one does on purpose, it just happens as you move through your everyday life. Plus, I knew if I let myself dwell on her too much, the guilt would overpower me. It was so much easier to bury those thoughts. Convincing myself that there was nothing else I could have done, I had to focus on my life for now. I didn't keep in touch like I should have either. I wish I could say that I called more and visited more often than I did, but I didn't. I was too focused on running from my own demons to think about the ones Angelee was still facing.

Angelee was still there, left to navigate the turmoil of her teenage years alone. That little girl with the long, curly hair and big, blue eyes was growing up in a world that still didn't seem to care much about her. And with nobody there to help guide her, she struggled to find her way. I wasn't aware of it back then, but our crazy childhood was leaving its mark on her, shaping her in ways that I couldn't have ever imagined.

The line between childhood and adulthood was starting to blur for her, and she was carrying the weight of it all in silence. While I wasn't there to see it all unfold personally, we did talk on the phone, and I heard stories, and I could guess. Day in and day out, home life was something Angelee had to survive, with no one to turn to for help.

CHAPTER 8:
DANDELIONS IN THE DARK

I was a long way from Grandma's home trying to carve out a new life for myself, but the distance didn't shield me from the nagging worry at the back of my mind, no matter how hard I tried to disregard it. The phone calls with Mom and the occasional home visits gave me just enough information to realize that things were changing—especially with Angelee. There were evident shifts in her that nobody fully understood.

Now, Angelee had always looked up to Mom and craved her approval as most any daughter does. It was like Mom was her compass, and Angelee would follow wherever that needle pointed. After I left, their bond seemed to grow stronger. She clung even tighter to Mom, despite her frequent absence, and was always hoping for a smile or some praise. Angelee saw in Mom what she wanted to believe was stability, a constant in life that was otherwise unpredictable. She latched to Mom like an anchor without me there to share the weight of all that chaos.

It was during this time that Angelee's moods started to shift in ways that were confusing. She was described as always being "moody" or "difficult." From my perspective, wasn't that just girls in general at that age? I didn't know. But Mom would tell me about how Angelee would be a whirlwind of energy, just overflowing with ideas and excitement. How she would talk rapidly about a new project or game. Her mind could be racing, her enthusiasm addictive. Later that same day, she'd sink into silence, every bit of her energy drained. It was as if something inside her had just been switched off without any warning.

She said it was like living with two different people sometimes, and it was impossible to keep up with it. The shifts were so unpredictable that she never knew how to respond. I would just chuckle and shake my head when I heard this. In hindsight, was it supposed to be clear these were signs of something deeper? But at that time, it was just one more layer of confusion in an already uproarious home.

There was one time I was on the phone with Mom and she shared a story that captured Angelee's shifting nature perfectly. She said it wasn't but a few weeks ago when this happened. It was a sunny, summer afternoon, and Mom was sitting in her favorite –spot—the old double wooden swing in the front yard. It really was a cool spot to just sit and swing. You had a perfect view of the park and playground across the street. It faced west, so you always got a great sunset.

I can picture her there with the rhythmic creaking of the swing, swaying back and forth in that gentle breeze. Those were her moments of peace. From her vantage point, she could see the kids playing on the swings and the monkey bars. That park was always our favorite place to play. There were so many memories there.

Mom supervised Angelee playing at the park with some friends. She was leading the group around all the playground equipment, up the slide, on the merry-go-round. Mom said they were so full of energy and laughter and that those kids were orbiting Angelee like the moon to the earth. Without warning, something out there shifted.

Angelee was giggling going down that slide, her cheeks flushed with joy. Then, when she was at the bottom, she stood up. Without a word, she wandered over to the crab apple trees that lined the parks edge. Mom watched as Angelee sat down with her back against the base of the tree, pulled her knees up to her chest, and sort of sank into the tree. Her vibrant demeanor was collapsing inwardly. Nothing happened, nobody was mad at her, she didn't seem mad; she had just suddenly withdrawn from everyone. As if the joy radiating from her moments before had disappeared.

I don't know why Mom didn't go over and check on her, but she said she sat there watching her for about twenty minutes, unsure of what to do. She couldn't tear her eyes away from Angelee, watching her curled up beneath that tree. Her body language was so different from the carefree kid she had just been. It was almost as if she was trying her best to hold herself together, but nobody knew why.

Then, just as quickly as the shift had come, Angelee stood up and walked away. She wandered beyond the playground over to the large field with tall grass. Mom said it was so interesting watching her go through the field and selectively pick dandelions—one, then another, and another. She was moving with purpose, but definitely without the spark she had earlier. Mom thought Angelee being up and moving around was a good sign. Angelee came home soon after, but something was still off about her.

Angelee silently passed Mom on the swing, her bouquet of dandelions in her hands. Their yellow heads were bright against the backdrop of Angelee's somber mood. She didn't really say much, just went to the kitchen and filled a small glass with water and carefully put the dandelions inside like they were fragile treasures. Mom said it was clear that these weren't just flowers to Angelee, that they held some deeper significance; Mom just didn't know what it was.

That evening, as the sun set and the house started to quiet down, she found Angelee in her room. I could hear the quiver in her voice as she described what she saw. Angelee was sitting in the dim light, her face was illuminated by the faint glow of the streetlight peeking between the crack of the curtains. She was staring at the dandelions, which were now starting to wilt in the glass. Their once bright flower heads were now sagging, just like her mood.

Mom stood there in the doorway, not quite sure what to do. She didn't want to intrude, but she felt helpless just standing there watching Angelee retreat into herself. She said it looked like Angelee had created a small world within those wilting dandelions. A small place where everything made sense to her, even if it didn't make sense to Mom. The weight of the unspoken sadness between them was a heavy feeling, and Mom didn't know how to bridge that gap.

The dandelions had seemingly become a metaphor for what was happening inside Angelee. One minute they were full of life, and the next they were fading, wilting under some unknown pressure. She sat there, hands wrapped gently around the glass as if it was the only thing keeping her tethered to the real world.

I sat speechless as I listened to Mom tell this story. Inside, I felt a deep sense of guilt. I wasn't there to see it. I wasn't there to help Angelee. I didn't understand what she was going through. I had distanced myself from that life, but in doing so, I had left Angelee behind to face her struggles alone.

Looking back, I realize how much those dandelions probably symbolized the fragile balance Angelee was trying to maintain. Just like those flowers, she was bright and full of potential, but the weight of life's unpredictability threatened to crush her spirit. Even though I had escaped, she was still there, grasping for something solid in a world that was constantly shifting beneath her feet.

CHAPTER 9: THE WEIGHT OF THE WORLD

The next morning, Angelee went to school, seemingly back to her usual self. Her animated persona was back in full force. She bounced out the door, her voice bubbling with excitement as she launched into a fun monologue about her new idea for some school project. Her words tumbled out faster than Mom's brain could process. It seemed almost impossible for her to contain that electric enthusiasm.

Mom sat at the dining room table, watching through that bay window, imagining how the day would unfold. Angelee would start out strong with super high energy and vibrant confidence. As the day progressed, however, Mom suspected her focus would start to wane.

It was a pattern Mom was becoming familiar with: starting the day with endless optimism only to be derailed by distractions. The behavior in classes would become erratic with each passing hour. She would be vivacious and talkative one moment, then distant and unfocused the next. Conversations would start lighthearted and energetic, only to come off the rails into awkward silences. It left people puzzled and even sometimes uncomfortable. That lively spirit that initially attracted people would soon leave them confused as they struggled to keep up with or understand the ever-changing tempo of her emotions.

Again, Mom only shared this with me because at home, Angelee's interactions were just as unpredictable, in a predictable way. Sometimes she would seek out intense closeness by curling up beside Mom. Angelee would crave reassurance with such a quiet and vulnerable voice. She sought out validation like it was a lifeline in those moments. Then just as quickly, she could retreat into her room and close the door, completely absorbing herself in drawing intricate pictures or reading whatever books she happened to have on hand. It was a stark contrast to the social and energetic girl she had been just hours earlier.

Mom did a great job painting a vivid picture of Angelee caught in a relentless cycle of emotional highs and lows. Her peaks were filled with laughter, creativity and connection. The lows came swiftly and intensely, and they cast long shadows over her previous joyfulness. The sudden shifts in her mood, her difficulties maintaining friendships, and her retreat into solitary activities hinted at a much deeper struggle. This is the storm she was battling beneath the surface.

There were other stories I heard or things I saw during my visits that make the difficulties she faced even clearer. They painted a picture that was both heartbreaking and overly confusing.

The hardest aspect of her life back then was her inability to maintain friendships. A revolving door of people who would enter her world, only to leave it just as quickly. It wasn't that Angelee had a hard time making friends, it was quite the opposite. She'd always had the ability to draw people in with her outgoing nature and alluring smile and enthusiasm. Forming those long-lasting connections was the challenge.

Middle school and high school were particularly brutal for her. Angelee was a strikingly beautiful girl. That long, curly, golden-blond hair that shimmered in the sunlight. Those gorgeous, piercing, blue eyes. this beauty should have been her armor, her shield. One would assume that these traits would have made her popular, the kind of girl others would admire. Instead though, it seemed her beauty became a source of ridicule. They would bully her by mocking her appearance, her clothes, even her demeanor. It wasn't admiration she was receiving, it was pure cruelty.

Mom shared with me about a time when Angelee wore a new dress to school. Well, it was a new dress to her. They'd bought it at the large, local thrift store, you know, the one that wasn't cool to shop at. They made a few alterations to the dress, trying to make it uniquely hers. She was so proud of this dress and walked into school with her head held high, only to be met with whispers and sneers. The other girls noticed, but they noticed it wasn't a brand-new dress, nor was it a name brand that was popular. It did not signal status. By the end of the day, Angelee's confidence was shattered, and she came home a mess—flushed cheeks, red eyes and tear-streaked cheeks. She refused to talk about what happened earlier in the day at school; the rejection of her peers had cut deep.

As the time passed, the lack of consistent friendships only deepened her turmoil.

Angelee's self-worth seemed to become entangled with how others treated her. The more she was bullied, the more isolated she became. She was caught in a cruel cycle, just yearning to fit in, but she was simultaneously pushing people away when they got close. When she did make new friends, she clung to them so intensely that it often overwhelmed them. And when they inevitably pulled away, that rejection cut deeper, fracturing her already fragile emotional state.

It was during those years that her mood swings became even more pronounced. Mom didn't understand what she was witnessing at that time, though. Angelee could be the life of the party, captivating those around her with her laughter and magnetic energy. Then, in a split second, she could retreat into herself, losing the spark in her eyes completely. Mom felt helpless, and I just kept asking, "Isn't this just a teenage girl?" Mom would just tell me no, that she was unsure how to reach Angelee when she seemed lost in her own world.

From what I understood, after everything we had been through and everything Angelee had survived once I'd left, high school was the absolute worst for her. She wasn't even able to make it to graduation. There was the turmoil within she was constantly fighting.

There was the bullying. The instability of friendships. The weight of her struggles became too much to bear. Angelee dropped out of high school in the tenth grade. Even with everything else, what truly broke her the day she left school not to return, was the incident with the one friend she had managed to hold onto. Someone she trusted completely. When that friend attempted to take their own life, it shattered Angelee in a way nothing else ever had. The devastation was unimaginable and suffocating.

That day, when Angelee walked out of high school, she didn't just leave behind her education, she also left a part of herself behind as well.

Having the benefit of hindsight, looking back now, it's painfully clear that Angelee's struggles went far beyond that of typical teenage angst. I often wonder if these had been early signs of something yet to come, or if understanding her better would have allowed us to reach her sooner. Before the scars of those early years had become too deep to heal.

CHAPTER 10: THE SHIFTING SANDS OF STABILITY

When Angelee left home and moved in with her boyfriend, I had high hopes that she might find some peace and some of the stability I had. Maybe she would find some semblance of the normalcy that had always eluded us growing up. Her transition into independent adulthood was far from smooth, though. She grappled with a series of odd jobs, each of them offering just enough to keep her afloat but never providing the security she desperately sought. Her life seemed like a perpetual balancing act. Her finances never quite aligned with her needs, which kept the ever-present certainty of her future just out of reach.

Her relationship with her boyfriend was tumultuous, often marked by a pattern of coming together and then falling apart. This on-again, off-again dynamic was a perfect mirror of the instability that had shadowed her life since childhood. When they were together, their relationship often teetered on the brink of disaster, only to end up unraveling again, leaving Angelee to pick up the pieces each time. Despite these upheavals, they did have two awesome boys both on the autism spectrum with Aspergers. Though each child presented unique challenges, one son was more functional than the other.

When they did finally decide to call it quits and move on with their lives separately, Angelee was left in a precarious situation. Alone with the boys, she faced the daunting task of raising them without the support of a partner. It was more than obvious that the pressure of her responsibilities was taking a toll on her. She did the best she could, nobody can deny that, but she did lean heavily on Mom and our aunt.

Their support was invaluable, providing a lifeline for Angelee and the boys. Mom helped the best she could, often stepping in to watch and care for the boys or to offer a listening ear when Angelee needed it the most. Our aunt had a professional background in special needs teaching. This allowed her to offer practical advice and a lot of hands-on help. The family support guided Angelee through the complexities of raising two children with needs.

During this time, Angelee's struggles were still evident. There were moments of relief when life seemed to stabilize, like when the boys were content and she'd managed to secure a steady, decent paying job. But these periods were often short lived. The pressures of managing her mental health, navigating all the demands of raising two children by herself, and maintaining relationships created a cycle of hope and despair. When life seemed to improve, it wasn't long before new challenges would arise, pulling her back into that same, familiar state of uncertainty.

In her personal life, Angelee seemed to have a continued need to seek companionship, causing her to move in and out of relationships. She had two long-term relationships during this time that I knew of, and they were each marked by their own set of challenges. Each partner brought a mix of support and strain into her life. These relationships were often characterized by a shared history of emotional highs and lows. They mirrored the pattern of instability that seemed to define Angelee's existence. This ebb and flow of the relationships provided temporary comfort, rarely lasting long enough to offer the stability she had always yearned for.

In each of these long-term relationships, the men truly cared for her. They treated her with kindness, supported her and the boys, and it really seemed as if they loved her deeply. Mom always thought, This might be the one. But inevitably, Angelee's troubles would resurface. I wasn't there much during these times, but from what I understood, the pressures of work, the demands of raising kids, or even just the inner turmoil she battled would begin to wear her down.

Even when she would decide she'd had enough and would terminate the relationship, these men would continue to love her from a distance. They would help with car payments, shuttling the boys from here to there, and even brought food around from time to time. They did this holding onto the hope that whatever demons she was fighting would eventually be conquered, and this would give them another chance to build a life with her. But eventually, they would finally reach their limit and move on.

Mom told me about a time Angelee had been dating someone new, but I don't remember who it was. Things had been going well until the argument. She had taken the boys to Mom's house to hang out for a bit and decompress. It wasn't long after they arrived when Mom noticed Angelee was missing. She found her out front, sitting alone on the old, wooden, double-seater swing, staring blankly at the setting sun across the park. Mom took a deep breath and went out to join her, taking a seat on the swing next to her. Angelee rested her head on Mom's shoulder, her eyes distant and red.

The boys were inside. You could occasionally hear them shouting and playing, but Angelee was lost in her thoughts. Angelee tried to put on a brave face for Mom's sake, but it was clear to Mom that something was bothering her, and whatever it was, was overwhelming. She told me how Angelee began to speak in fragmented sentences, that her words were a jumble of frustration, sadness, and confusion. It was as if she was trying to articulate the chaos within herself, yet was incapable of finding the right words. Angelee just kept saying, "I just don't understand why life is so hard."

Even with the unwavering support from Mom and our aunt and the brief stability offered by her relationships, Angelee remained ensnared in this relentless cycle. One of hope and disappointment. Each time she would take some steps forward, new obstacles seemed to appear and drag her right back. Her mental health, that constant, looming presence, was a significant factor in this ongoing struggle. The same unpredictability that had always characterized her childhood continued to shadow her into adulthood. It left her life as turbulent and unstable as ever.

Angelee's struggles were deeply interconnected with her past, a web that was impossible to untangle. The challenges of her childhood, the instability of her upbringing and the weight of her adult responsibilities had woven together into a tapestry of hardship and resilience. The invisible, underlying issues remained constant.

CHAPTER 11: REDISCOVERING DREAMS

One of Angelee's biggest dreams was that of owning her own home, a place she could truly call hers. I can't remember the exact year, but I'll never forget the day she finally made that dream a reality. She had somehow been scrimping and saving for quite some time and was finally able to buy a beautiful, three-bedroom house. It was close to Mom's, maybe a five-minute drive, which was perfect! Angelee was, as expected, over the moon about it. She was actually glowing when she told me.

Not long after she moved in, I was able to go visit her and the boys. I could see why she was so proud. The house was perfect for them. A cozy, two-story house with its own huge backyard that was fenced in for the dog. It was on a quiet, well-kept street with friendly neighbors and a sense of peace that made it feel like she had finally found the stability she so desperately sought for so long.

Inside, the house was immaculate. Everything was clean and in perfect order, reflecting how much care and effort she had put into making this place a real home—her home. The boys each had their own bedrooms, something she had always wanted for them. You could see just how much joy it brought her to give that to them.

There was something almost magical about seeing Angelee so happy. Standing there in the doorway of her very own house with her dog at her feet, smiling ear to ear like she'd finally made it to a place where life wasn't so hard. It was one of those moments that sticks with you, a rare glimpse of peace in what always had been so turbulent.

Having achieved this dream brought to the forefront another part of her life that remained unsettled: her education. Dropping out in the tenth grade and leaving behind the dreams that she once held dear had haunted her for years. She had never let go of those aspirations, they were still there, tucked away in the corner of her heart, nagging from time to time, just waiting to be reignited. That time had almost arrived.

At this point, Angelee was dating one of her long-term boyfriends, a man who saw the potential in her and encouraged her to revisit this dream. He knew how much it bothered her having the unfinished business of high school. With his unwavering support, Angelee made the brave decision to realize that dream of graduating. She was going back to earn her GED.

While it may have been an intimidating decision, and she did have a little hesitation in her voice when she first told me about it, she went all in. The self-doubt that was lingering after all those years lifted easily away when she committed. The old Angelee, the one who always fought against the odds, had reemerged. Confidence and pride could be heard in her voice when she told us her intentions of reclaiming something she'd thought had been lost forever. For the first time is such a long while, it felt like things were finally falling into place for her. She was pushing forward, hard and fast. We were all so proud.

She accomplished that goal and realized that dream. She got her GED. Then came the next announcement, one that was truly amazing! With her GED in hand, she announced that she wasn't stopping there. She was going to college. And she wasn't going to study just any program, she wanted to study something meaningful. Something that would help her understand and support her boys better. Those boys were her world, and she wanted to do everything in her power to be the best mom she could be.

She enrolled in college with a clear goal in mind: to earn a degree in Liberal Arts. It wasn't just about the college degree, this field fascinated her deeply. She believed it would equip her with the tools she needed to better understand the unique challenges her boys faced. Angelee wasn't doing this solely for herself; she was driven by the deep-seated desire to help her sons in a way that had the ability to profoundly impact their lives.

Once she started, she poured herself into those studies so intensely that it left all of us in awe. She was doing it, my little sister, the one who had been through so much in life. The dedication to her coursework was incredible. She spoke passionately about some of the things she was learning. The ideas that opened new ways of thinking for her. Creative problem solving, tolerance, self-awareness, and respect. These were not just abstract concepts to her. She wasn't just surviving anymore, Angelee was thriving in a way that was so much fun to watch, even if it was from a distance.

She spoke of how what she was learning was helping her see the world, and even her own family, through a different lens. She had learned to approach situations with so much more patience and was developing new strategies to cope with everyday challenges. This education wasn't just about academic pursuit for her; it was becoming a tool for personal growth, a way for her to carve out a new, brighter future for herself and her family.

That enthusiasm was far more than contagious. That light in her eyes, I hadn't seen that is so many years. Life was stabilizing for her, and it was about time. She had leveled up in life. She found something that gave her a sense of accomplishment and direction. Something that made her believe she could overcome anything in her path. And watching her dive headfirst into those studies, I believed it too.

The day she graduated from college was one of the proudest moments of my life. While I wasn't able to be there in person, the picture she'd sent me captured everything. I can still see it when I close my eyes now: Angelee standing in front of the college, her boys flanking her on either side, and that damn smile—it was huge! It was the kind of smile that radiated pure joy and happiness. A smile that told the story of victory, of resilience, and mostly, of love.

I couldn't have been any prouder. Seeing her there, that diploma in hand, knowing exactly the journey she had taken to get to that moment. It filled me completely with happiness. Angelee had done it; she had reclaimed her life, her dreams and her future. And even though I wasn't there to see it in person, that picture and the emotions it had captured are etched into my memory forever. My little sister. Stronger than ever. I couldn't be happier.

CHAPTER 12: MOM'S DEATH AND THE AFTERMATH

September 2013 marked a profound turning point in my life. It was a month that remains seared into my memory with the clarity of an unshakable, vivid dream. The days leading up to my mom's death were a blur of worry, fatigue and an imposing sense of impending loss. Mom had dealt with illness for the majority of her life in one form or another. But as her condition deteriorated, it was painfully clear that her body had become too frail and was no longer capable of withstanding the unyielding assault from years of medical conditions and disease. She'd spent her final days in that hospital room, the sanctuary of sorrow. Its atmosphere was punctuated by the soft beeping of all the medical monitors and the subdued murmurs of our family members. This symphony of sounds became the backdrop of our collective grief.

Mom's health history was an extensive chronicle of suffering. Kidney disease was the culprit of her first kidney being removed at the age of sixteen, a blow that started it all. In 2002, when she lost her second kidney, that's when she started the process of dialysis. It was a constant reminder of a terminal diagnosis. Her struggles didn't stop there, though. She fought breast cancer, endured a flesh-eating virus that ravaged her upper thighs, and even had open heart surgery to address a heart valve failure.

Despite the relentless barrage of medical challenges, our mom possessed a rare and formidable strength. She fought harder than any doctor ever thought she was capable of. Yet even the strongest of spirits can falter under such an immense pressure, and it was all this weight for so long, that finally proved to be just too much for her. The day before she passed away, she told me, "I'm just so tired, Joe. Please let it be ok if I go. I'm so tired of always being in pain." It was just over a week before my birthday.

One of the most heart wrenching moments in my life was when Angelee called that September. Her voice pierced through the line, strained and urgent. "Joe, you need to get up here. The doctors say that mom only has one or two days left." Those words, they hit hard. One or two days. For a minute, I stood there, frozen with the phone stuck to my ear. I was struggling for my brain to catch up with the words my ears had heard. It was almost like the world outside the phone call went silent, shrinking to just that moment between Angelee's voice and my heartbeat.

I wanted to believe it was just another false alarm, just another scare and that Mom would pull through again. She had survived so much before. This time, however, there was something in Angelee's voice—maybe a tremble, a slight hesitation, I don't know—that told me this was different. The cold sweat that was settling on my skin told me the same thing.

They were five hundred miles away from my home here in Tennessee. Right then, in that instant, everything felt so distant and irrelevant. The thought of not being there, of not being able to hold Mom's hand and tell her I love her one last time was unbearable.

Anxiety was gnawing at me, and the fear of time slipping away was imminent.

I grabbed a small suitcase from my closet, and I realized my hands were trembling as I threw in a few shirts. I wasn't paying too much attention to what I was packing. The smell of freshly washed laundry mixed with the faint, stale smell of the closet hit my nose, but it all felt –distant, like I was on autopilot. My thoughts were still stuck on the call.

As I finished throwing a few things in the suitcase, it hit me that it had been months since Angelee and I had spoken last, at least about anything other than Mom's health. Time had again swept by into the same of routine of everyday life. My chest tightened as I looked over at my phone, hoping it would ring again to tell me it was all just a mistake.

Everyone gathered around Mom's bed as her final days approached. Each hour felt like an eternity that I didn't want to end. The weight of our despair made the small room feel suffocating. Family members filled the room, sharing stories about Mom and attempting to engage with her.

Angelee was the most profoundly affected by what was happening. Her face resembled a picture of exhaustion and devastation. Her eyes, so bright and full of hope in the past, were now hollowed even further by pure fear. She had always been the one to help Mom through her health crises.

I can remember the first summer Mom went on dialysis. While the rest of us struggled to wrap our heads around what happened, it was Angelee who stepped up. She'd sit with Mom by her side during most every session. She would hold her hand and talk her through the worst of it. I saw them together in the hospital room, their heads bent close as they shared quiet words that no one else could hear. Mom was leaning on Angelee in a way she hadn't ever leaned on anyone else. And now, I sat there watching Angelee hold Mom's hand for what was probably the last time. It was like she wasn't just losing her best friend or her closest confidant, but she was losing the person who had always needed her the most.

It was right there, at that single moment in time, seeing Angelee cradle Mom's hand and cry silently because she was all out of tears, that for some strange reason, I thought about the fact that I never knew if Mom had picked out a song for her and Angelee. I didn't know that my heart was capable of breaking any further, but it broke even further at that the possibility of there never having been a shared song between them.

Angelee's fingers trembled, and Mom's breaths were short and shallow, ragged gasps. The entire room was filled with the hushed sobs of everyone. The incessant hum of the machines and the crushing silence of our shared grief was overpowering. The soft, rhythmic beeping of those machines were a constant during those final days. Steady, predictable, and anything but comforting.

When Mom's breathing finally ceased, the world came to a standstill. Losing Mom crushed every ounce of everything in our worlds. The room was shrinking and the walls were closing in somehow as the finality of her death became undeniable. The beeping had stopped. The silence was deafening.

The funeral that followed was a somber affair. It was the gathering of family and friends who had all been touched by Mom's life. There were so many people there. The funeral was adorned with an abundance of flower bouquets of vibrant colors that contrasted sharply with the somber mood of the occasion. The air was heavy with the scent of lilies and the murmurs of condolences. It was the classic atmosphere of mourning and reflection; it was a beautiful service.

Angelee was hit the hardest by Mom's death. She dissolved into her grief, losing the essence of the lively, though troubled, person she had once been. This loss left her adrift in tumultuous emotions. Watching her there, I couldn't hide the pang of guilt I felt. I hadn't noticed exactly how much distance had grown between the two of us. We had lived in different worlds for so long that the years actually blurred together. I told myself that she was my sister, and she was as strong as I was, that it was ok. She would be ok. But her reactions were raw and unfiltered, a very poignant reflection of the deep emotional turmoil that was holistically consuming her.

In the weeks that followed the funeral, Angelee retreated from everyone. She quit answering phone calls even from our aunt, who had been a pillar of support for so long. She endured self-imposed exile from the very people who were her closest allies. We all believed, at first, that she was simply withdrawing as a way of processing and coping with the unimaginable grief. She just needed time. But as time kept passing, it was starting to become clear that there was something more troubling at play. Angelee seemed to be unraveling, and despite our best efforts, none of us were able to reach her. She had literally disappeared.

It was about three months after I returned home from Mom's funeral when my phone rang. I was outside on the tractor, moving some dirt or something at the time. It was Angelee calling. As soon as I answered the phone, her voice shattered the peacefulness of the moment. She erupted into a frantic torrent of incoherent yelling. Her words tumbled out of her mouth in a chaotic mess of anger and agony. What she said barely made sense, but it was full of intense, raw emotion. She was yelling something about Mom's death, and the distress in Angelee's voice was evident even though the specifics were lost in the confusion. This phone call felt like a violent storm of sound, completely mirroring her overwhelmed state and deep turmoil. It left me grappling with a profound sense of helplessness and confusion.

I was still reeling and fighting my own emotions, and this frantic call only added to my own sense of frustration. Unfortunately, my response was impatient and curt, as I was unable to mask the edge of my own unresolved anger. I cut her off when I spoke up. "Angelee, you need to calm down," I snapped, my voice tight with frustration. "We need to talk about this later. I'm still struggling with all of this myself, and I don't even know what you're talking about." My feeble attempt to manage my own grief while dealing with her outburst only seemed to deepen the divide between us. It left me feeling even more helpless and disconnected than before. The call ended with her saying, "You no longer have a sister." Then the line went dead.

The way I saw it, the anger Angelee directed towards me felt irrational, likely a reaction rooted in her own ongoing struggle to process Mom's death. I understood that her emotions were tangled in confusion and sadness, and I knew that she had the support of her boys, my aunt, and her boyfriend. Once she was ready to talk, I would be there to answer the phone, but she had to cool down first.

Still, I was worried. I'd never heard her speak like that before. I reached out to my cousin and asked her if she could try to check in on Angelee. I explained what happened and why I was concerned. Agreeing, she said she would try to reach her, hoping to offer some sort of comfort in such a distressful time.

If I had only known then what I know now, I would have dropped everything and gone to Michigan to be there for her. But I was consumed with my own anguish, stuck trying to sort through Mom's death in my own way. It never occurred to me that Angelee's outburst may have been a cry for help.

Life has a way of pulling you in so many directions—raising kids, going to work, managing the everyday workflow and stresses—that sometimes you don't always notice just how much time has passed since you last connected with someone. Before you know it, years slip by, unnoticed and unrecoverable. Seven years went by without a word from or about Angelee. All I knew was that she had moved up north with her boyfriend and the boys.

Then out of the blue, on March 18, 2021, I finally received an update.

CHAPTER 13: THE DAY MY WORLD CHANGED FOREVER

It was a predictable Thursday evening, a routine we had come to enjoy after a long, stressful day of work. My wife and I had finished supper hours ago and were both in our favorite spots in the living room. I was enjoying a glass of bourbon from a new distillery that a friend had recommended as the dialog of some television show flickered in the background. We were content with the stillness of the evening, until my phone rang.

It jarred me from my thoughts as I looked over to see who it was. It was my cousin, and normally at this hour, I would just allow it to go to voicemail as I continued to decompress from the day. I'm not sure if it was some feeling I had, or maybe the oddness of the hour she was calling, or because I was looking for a distraction from whatever I was thinking about, but I swiped the little bar on the screen and answered.

"Hello?"

"Joey," she said, her voice trembling as if she didn't want to tell me why she'd called. I felt it immediately, some weight of the unknown. Just the way she said it formed a knot in my chest. She continued, "Joey, Angelee is in trouble… She's been arrested. She killed Bill."

The world around me froze in place. My heart pounded so hard that I could feel it in my throat. It was a heavy, insistent thudding. Was I about to vomit? For a moment I felt lightheaded, as though the ground beneath had shifted.

"What?" I asked, my voice barely above a whisper and full of disbelief and confusion. Time stopped as those words—Angelee, arrested, killed—were suspended in my mind. It just didn't make sense.

I heard her repeat the same words, each one a blow that I wasn't prepared for. Angelee had been arrested for killing her boyfriend and his two dogs. My head shook. I sat there, stunned, desperately trying to get my mind to grasp an explanation. The TV, the bourbon, the silence that had just been all faded into a blur in the distance. "I don't understand, what happened? Angelee?" My voice cracked, barely able to get the words out.

She said that she didn't know what happened, and she repeated the same words. There was no escaping the truth of what she'd said, I'd heard them correctly.

Angelee had always been the gentle one. The one who cared for everyone, humans and animals alike. Hurting someone was beyond unimaginable. Just the thought of her harming another human being left me paralyzed in disbelief. How in the world could this be the same person who was the first to help someone in need? For as long as I can remember it was Angelee that always saw the good in people, even when no one else could. Trying to reconcile the thought of her taking a life, Bill's life, was impossible.

The memories of her kindness and warmth were starting to flood my mind. I saw the little girl who would stop and give the homeless guy a dollar if she had one, even if it was her only one. She was the one who spoke of love over hate. She believed that no matter how broken someone was, they could be saved. She believed so deeply in the goodness of humanity. How could she harm someone?

And the dogs, too? What in the holy hell is going on? Her beloved animals? I thought back to all the strays she would bring home, her face glowing with each animal she rescued. How she nurtured them back to health and loved on them. Her entire world would stop if she saw an animal in need. She had dedicated so much of her life to helping animals and protecting them. It just wasn't making any sense. The shockwaves were tearing through me. All while I sat motionless, the phone still pressed to my ear.

My cousin kept talking, but I wasn't hearing a word she said. I hung up in the middle of her speaking, not intentionally, it just happened. How could this be the same person? This question kept reverberating in my mind. And there was no answer for it.

I looked over at my wife who was sitting there, looking at me with concern etched into her face. Though Angelee and my wife had never met, my wife felt she had a sense for my sister through all the stories I've told. Whenever we were out and I saw a stray at the gas station or wherever, I'd always say the same thing, jokingly but honestly. "Good thing Angelee isn't with us. We'd be waiting here all day for her to save that thing." My wife knew Angelee to be a kind, caring and gentle person, but also one who had become sad and lost after our mom passed. My wife's response was one of disbelief as well. Her heart poured out to my sister, but I could see a deeper sadness. A sadness for the version of Angelee I described, and for the version of Angelee that had been lost in this darkness.

It was impossible to sleep that night. I laid there for hours staring at the ceiling. Those thoughts just kept looping endlessly in a haze. How? How could this have happened? What are we missing? I couldn't get the vision of Angelee's face out of my mind, or at least the version of who she had been. No matter how hard things got, she always held onto the belief of the good in people. She loved Bill.

They had met at a shared workplace. There isn't a lot of detail I have about their lives together; the seven-year gap left a lot to wonder. One thing I do know is that she was so happy with him. He seemed to be able to help her work through the grief of Mom's passing. He shared his love of motorcycles with her, she gushed about him and how grateful she was to have someone like him in her life. And those dogs, their dogs. Angelee would have moved mountains for her dogs.

These memories of her, of who she had been, kept burning through my mind as I lay there staring at the ceiling. They kept clashing violently with the reality I was now being forced to accept. No matter how many times I tried to make sense of it, I just couldn't. The more I thought about it, the blurrier it became, and the confusion was suffocating. I always circled back and was left with the same impossible question: How could this have happened?

CHAPTER 14: THE ROAD TO UNCERTAINTY

When the morning finally arrived, the shock still clung to me. The morning light was just beginning to stream through the gap in the bedroom curtains. I rolled over and saw my wife staring at me, her eyes wide and tired. It was clear she'd had a rough night and that sleep had eluded her as well. We didn't need to say anything, the silence said enough. We got out of bed and began the day, both of us unaware of what lay ahead.

Unlike most mornings where drinking coffee was a comfortable routine, that morning felt anything but normal or reassuring. We both stared at our half-empty coffee cups, the silence stretching between us. Neither of us really knew what to say. There was an odd feel to the air in the kitchen that morning as the uncertainty hung heavily.

I could see that her hands were gripping the coffee mug a little tighter than usual. "We need to go, you know this," she said, her low voice breaking the uneasy silence. Her eyes were searching mine, looking for some kind of reassurance, something to cling to. But we both knew that wasn't something I could give her in that moment. I did, however, manage to nod my head; my throat was too tight to let words escape. Hell, even if I could have spoken, I didn't want to. Anything I could have said would only make everything feel more real.

Bottom line was, she was right. We did need to go, to be there for Angelee's boys. We needed to be with family to face the reality of what happened and somehow help navigate this nightmare.

Those thoughts felt unreal though, even as they formed in my mind. It felt like I was completely detached from my own life and was drifting through someone else's tragedy. How in the hell could we help anyone when we weren't even sure how to get through this ourselves? How did it come to this, finding myself facing the unimaginable truth that my own little sister had done something beyond comprehension?

The drive north was anything but easy; each mile seemed to stretch on so much further than the last. We were passing all the familiar landmarks and scenery, but none of it really registered. My mind was miles away, lost in a swirling mix of emotions. The fear, anger and helplessness was constantly stinging. My wife and I would occasionally exchange glances or manage to force out a few words just trying to make conversation, but it didn't really help much. It was a grueling tension, not because of anything that was said or not said, just because of the uncertainly that was in front of us.

As we got closer to the Michigan state line, my thoughts turned to Bill. I hadn't known him very well, only having met him twice, but those two interactions were all that was needed for him to make a great impression. I saw the way he interacted with Angelee—he was kind, respectful and had a genuine fondness for her. When I met him, they had just been spending time together, not officially dating. There was a way he looked at her, though, with an admiration that spoke volumes.

To me, he came across as genuinely humble. He spoke with respect, and we shared more than a few laughs that night. We were able to connect over a mutual love of the outdoors, riding motorcycles and tinkering around—him with cars, me in the wood shop. The way he treated Angelee said more than enough about his character. I had no doubt in my mind that if things progressed into a relationship between them, he would be good to her.

Now he was gone. The finality of it felt like a kick from a horse. He had been a steady and reassuring presence in her life. None of it made any sense to me.

The emotional odyssey of the drive was hard to find words for. Every mile brought us closer to the reality I wasn't ready to face, a monstrous truth that was too horrifying to accept. My mind kept circling back to those words on the phone call, to the shock and disbelief I'd felt hearing them. I could still hear her voice loud and clear, the resignation in her words, the tremor in her voice when she told me the news.

Angelee killed Bill.

The weight of what awaited us was starting to settle deep into my bones. I wanted to wake up, wishing somebody would just call my phone and tell me it was just a horrible mistake, that they'd misunderstood what they heard. But the phone never rang, and I was already painfully awake.

We were very close to Wayne when my wife, staring straight ahead, quietly asked, "What about the boys? They have to be so scared and confused." I replied the only way I knew how, "I'm not sure. I haven't seen them in years either."

Angelee's sons were both young adults now, both subtly suffering from Asperger's syndrome. They were super high functioning and held above average intelligence, but that didn't stop us from worrying and wondering how were they handling the news and what they must be feeling.

This wasn't just about Angelee anymore, it was about all of us. The family. Bill. The boys. Our lives were now irrevocably changed, completely shattered by the reality of the unthinkable. There was no going back; no do-overs. The echoes of that phone call had left a mark on me that would remain for the rest of my life.

CHAPTER 15:
A FAMILY IN SHADOWS

When we finally arrived, most of the family was already there at the park across from Grandma's old house. The park had changed so much, I couldn't recognize it. All the playground equipment we spent our childhood on was gone. It was replaced by beautiful baseball fields, all surrounded by their own chain-link fence with banners advertising local businesses I'd never heard of. In the middle of the fields, there was a massive, two-story building with concessions at the bottom. That building stood where the merry-go-round used to be. The old ice-skating rink, which was nothing more than a spot in the field that would flood and freeze over during the winter, was now a parking lot.

It was this new parking lot that we pulled into and saw our family waiting. Such a strange disorientation consumed me. Everything looking so different made me feel like the years had just wiped away all those memories I had of this place, my childhood sanctuary. It was unrecognizable, foreign almost. Even the old crab apple trees were gone. And like the playground that I once cherished had disappeared, the sister I once knew had changed just as much.

Dread filled the air as we walked over to greet everyone. They were gathered beneath some big, new pavilion that had a bunch of picnic tables. Instead of the typical family reunion with cheerful greetings, all we saw was solemn faces and quiet angst. We all hugged, but those hugs came with tears and choked sobs as people tried and failed to hold back their tears.

Everyone was lost, even in such a familiar place. Everyone's expressions were heavy with the weight of the unknown. What really happened? Why? How? What happens next? Nobody knew the answers.

"What do we do now?" my elderly aunt asked through the tears streaming down her face. All the familiar faces I'd grown up with now all looked haunted and lost. Everyone was looking for some kind of clarity, some answers in the midst of the unknown.

After the initial wave of emotions started to settle, we spent the majority of the afternoon talking, speculating, worrying. During the silence between conversations, I found myself looking over at Grandma's house more than once. It stood there steadfast; and there was that damned old, double-wood swing. It was dilapidated now, though. It didn't appear safe enough for anyone to even sit on. What was it still doing there?

Grandma's house was a distant echo of the past. So many memories were rooted in that one piece of property where life seemed simpler, almost safe. And now, it was nothing more than a relic from the past.

The conversations that day went nowhere. We just didn't know what to do. Nobody had any answers, just that deep sense of uncertainty. My cousin was the only one who had been able to talk to Angelee's public defender, but even that conversation didn't reveal much. It was so frustrating. That gathering simply left everyone with more questions than answers.

- As the days stretched into weeks, and the weeks turned into months, nothing changed. The attorney was keeping all the information held close. We were learning more from the news articles than anything, and that wasn't much at all. We weren't able to move forward, and it was way too early for any closure. Every phone call, every email was the same, nothing was new.

And so we waited, clinging to any fresh bit of information that may have come.

We waited. We worried. We wondered. We cried.

Then one day, a few months after we'd met in the park, Angelee's attorney called me. She stated that Angelee wanted to call me, but she warned me not to discuss the case at all. Not just because there was an ongoing investigation, but because her mental health was still very fragile. Talking about the specifics could cause more harm than good.

Over the course of that year, from finding out about the arrest to the start of the hearing, Angelee called me twice. The first time was more than painfully awkward. When she called the first time, I didn't recognized the number. I thought it might have been work related or a telemarketer. When I answered and heard her voice, my stomach knotted. Every bit of air was instantly sucked out of the room. The wave of nausea that came over me was powerful. I wanted to hang up almost instantly to escape that shock of hearing her on the other end, but I couldn't. I wouldn't.

Her voice was very hesitant, timid. It was as if she was forcing herself to make a call she was afraid to make.

"Joe. It's your sister. How are you?" Her voice was fragile and small, as if she was holding back everything else she was wanting to say.

"I'm doing as well as can be expected, Angelee," I replied, trying hard to keep my voice steady. So many emotions hit me all at once, but I knew I had to push them back down. I had so many questions burning to be asked, questions I knew that I couldn't ask.

Then came something I wasn't expecting at all. She asked, "Do you hate me now?"

That gut punch. Of all the things she should have been worried about, this is what she needed to know. My chest tightened and my heart sank. I wanted to speak, but my throat was dry, and for a moment, I just couldn't find any words. I was gripping the phone tighter with shaking hands. I knew I had to steady myself.

The weight of that question, the fact that she even had to ask, made me feel sick. I was on the verge of losing everything I thought I knew.

I took a deep breath and answered cautiously, "I'm confused, Angelee. No, I don't hate you, but I do hate what happened. I'm worried about you. I love you, but there's just so much I don't understand."

She appeared to find some level of comfort in my words. We continued the conversation. It remained heavy and elusive. We spoke about the boys, some of the family members, and I, of course, asked if she needed anything. Then, out of nowhere, she said, "Joe, I killed Bill. At least that's what they tell me. I don't remember anything."

Those words hung in the air, each and every syllable landing like a rock dropped into a still pond. I couldn't get my mind to catch up, to understand exactly what she just said. I wanted to ask more, to press her for further details, but I knew I couldn't. As my heart raced and I felt the tension in my shoulders tighten, I realized I was gripping the phone so tight that my hand was cramped.

There was an urge to confront her, but I was hung up on the sheer horror of her confession. It was then that somehow, I reminded her we weren't supposed to talk about the case. Even as I said those words, I knew they sounded so hollow. It wasn't just a case, it was our lives. So many people had been shattered in ways that I was still trying to comprehend. She apologized as her voice broke into soft sobs. I wanted so badly to reach right through that phone and somehow pull her out of this nightmare we were all living in. But I couldn't. And as much as I wanted to get off the phone, I also didn't want to let her go.

Those emotions, in that moment in time, were overwhelming. Part of me wanted to end the call, as I was afraid to keep talking, afraid of what else I might hear that would make it somehow more real in an irreversible way. The other part of me never wanted the call to end, to just be able to continue trying to give her some sort of comfort. But I didn't even know how to comfort myself.

CHAPTER 16: FACING THE DARKNESS

A penetrating sense of dread was settling over me as the hearing drew closer. There was an unexplainable pull that was overpowering me to attend, to be there for Angelee. The emotions inside were difficult to even understand, let alone deal with. It was a whirlwind of feelings. I still had quite a bit of fierce anger towards her for all the havoc she'd created. Not just for our family, but for those of Bill's family too. Even with such pointed anger, there was a deep, abiding sorrow lingering in my heart for her. My little sister was confined to a jail cell, staring down a future of complete uncertainty. Those feelings were polarizing. And then there was a weird, strange bittersweet feeling of relief. I was so happy Mom had been spared from being able to witness this tragedy unfold. Seeing her beloved daughter ensnared in such dire circumstances would have been unbearable.

My feelings and thoughts were all shifting constantly; ebbing and flowing like the tide, only much quicker. It was impossible to grapple with the harsh reality of the situation. Despite those fluctuating and confusing emotions, I knew I needed to be there for Angelee. Even with the enormity of her actions, and how they had impacted so many lives.

Over the last couple of days before the hearing, I tried to prepare for what lay ahead. The tension was insufferable. Whenever I found myself thinking about going, which was all the time, I could feel my heart beating faster, my breathing getting shallower. Sleep was unreachable; I spent the whole night tossing and turning, terrified of the weight pressing down on me. The tension that had been in my shoulders became physical pain that radiated in my neck. Everything was a constant reminder of the anxiety that had taken hold of me.

One of my adult sons had decided to make the trip with me up to Manistee, Michigan for the hearing. This drive was grueling and unrelenting. The stress we felt was crystalized within that car for the entire trip. Those roads stretched endlessly, and oddly enough, they mirrored the insecurity and apprehension we were both feeling. We didn't discuss much about the actual reason we were headed north.

There was one point where my son broke the silence by asking, "How do you think she's doing?" There was a sadness in his voice that I wasn't used to hearing.

"I don't know" was my honest reply. I never looked up from the road. "I really don't know."

The humming of the tires on the pavement was the only sound we heard after that conversation. My son was very supportive, but I could feel the burden of his own conflict. Neither of us knew exactly what to expect, and the unknown pressed down on both of us.

We got to that small town later in the evening, checked into our hotel and decided to grab a bite to eat. Looking for a brief respite, we found a local dive bar. I figured we could hide amongst the locals and enjoy a burger and a cold beer. And for a couple hours that night, we were able to talk, hidden in the murmurs of conversation in that bar.

Sure enough, as soon as we got back to the hotel that night, the courthouse loomed large in my mind again. The brevity of relief I had felt slipped right away, replaced with the cold, hard reality of what was waiting for us in the morning.

A quick breakfast provided in the lobby was all we grabbed before heading out that morning. We arrived at the courthouse well before the hearing was scheduled to begin. A small crowd had gathered outside the doors, likely Bill's friends and family. Their presence cast a long shadow over our arrival. The sight of them made me feel exposed and amplified the dread even further. I felt like an intruder and was painfully aware of how they might perceive us. It was in that moment that I desperately wanted to just turn around and leave. My only desire was to avoid the confrontation I was certain awaited us.

We sat in the car for quite some time. Our unspoken fears created a silence we were becoming more comfortable with. People started to enter the courthouse, and our hearts sank with each passing figure. The vicious storm of emotions began swirling around within me again, but my son was a steadying presence. I looked over at him, my voice thick with gratitude when I said, "Thank you for being here, son. I love you, and I'm sorry we have to go through this."

He looked me straight in the eyes, his gaze full of understanding. "Dad, I'm glad I'm here with you. We'll get through this."

Even though his words were simple, they were perfect for my troubled heart. But beneath the comfort provided by his words loomed a layer of guilt I just couldn't shake. Guilt for having dragged him into this mess. He shouldn't have had to experience this, and yet, there we were.

Entering the courthouse made me yearn for the bar again. I questioned my decision to make this trip in the first place. The building held that certain small-town charm—quaint and picturesque—but the moment we passed through those front doors, it felt imposing and frightening. As we walked up to the metal detectors and emptied our pockets, the deputy asked us the reason for our visit. I hesitated and then with a shaky voice muttered, "The Ross hearing."

We opted to take the stairs to the second floor over the elevator. I wanted to ensure we avoided any potential encounters with his family in an elevator. The climb up those stairs was arduous, each step loudly amplifying my fears. When we reached the top of the stairs, it opened up into a large hallway filled with the sight of well-dressed people and uniformed officers, which somehow intensified my unease.

Inside the courtroom itself, COVID protocols had reduced the seats in the gallery to just about fifteen seats. They were spread out and mostly already occupied, presumably with Bill's family and friends. Their stares were noticeable; they were trying to determine who we were and where did we fit into this scenario. Each gaze was a stinging reminder of the pain Angelee had inflicted.

I wanted to speak, to say something, anything, to apologize. Maybe offer some sort of solace, but there were no words that could help ease the pain they were feeling. My throat was tight, and the guilt of what my sister did was heavy in my chest. I felt exposed, as if I didn't belong in that room. I was intruding on their grief.

The defense attorney was a distinguished woman who had a dignified air about her. With purposeful steps, she walked directly over to us. I felt targeted, and it was a very unnerving feeling. She introduced herself with a calm, steady voice and correctly identifying me as Joe, Angelee's brother. While there was empathy in her eyes, her tone remained very matter-of-fact. As though she had been through this process countless times before. Her professionalism was clear. It was evident that she knew how to navigate these situations. But we didn't, and we were struggling to manage the emotional landscape we found ourselves in.

The defense attorney thanked us for being there for Angelee, but she wanted to caution us that the day ahead would be incredibly difficult. At this point, I truly realized the extent of our exposure. There was no mistaking who we were now. The eyes of the entire gallery were fixed on us. We were the family of the woman who had caused them so much pain. I was embarrassed beyond anything. Regret washed over me entirely. That wish I had to retreat was stronger now than I had ever felt in my life.

PART II
THE HEARING

CHAPTER 17:
A SISTER IN CHAINS

Out in the hall, Angelee's attorney briefed us. She prepared us as best she could for the testimonies that we would hear that day. The clinical way in which she spoke was jarring. Everything she said were just facts to be processed.

There were a lot of people lined up to testify: laypersons, first responders and state troopers. Each of them would be telling their versions of what they experienced. She warned us that what we were about to hear would be difficult to understand, both emotionally and logically. For us, though, I felt that each testimony would deepen the wound from the previous testimony. I was nervous. My heart was racing yet again, wondering what exactly we would hear. What details would be revealed? What truths were we so unprepared for?

The courtroom was shrouded in a heavy, almost oppressive silence. It was that kind of suffocating silence that seemed to amplify everything—every emotion, every breath. Occasionally the quiet was broken by the faint whispers between the attorneys, though they were barely even audible. Then came the moment that drastically shifted the entire atmosphere. They brought Angelee in.

Seeing her in that grey jumpsuit with an orange jacket slung over her shoulders was shocking and unsettling. The sight of her shackled in handcuffs and chains around her ankles knocked the wind out of me. She looked sad, disheveled, and lost. Her hair was in disarray and her total appearance was such a stark contrast to the vibrant sister I remembered and, for some reason, expected to see here. She shuffled forward with the help of the bailiff, her eyes remained fixated on the ground as she moved. Was she this lost or was she making a conscience effort not to make eye contact with anyone?

Then, all of a sudden, it happened, and it happened so quick. She looked right at me. It was as if I was the only one there, as if she had known exactly where I was sitting. The look she gave me was one I had never seen from her before. Quizzical, perhaps tinged with shame or embarrassment. Hell, maybe it was anger, I don't know. It was something completely new. But it was a gaze that defied any interpretation and left me momentarily paralyzed. I couldn't hold her gaze and instinctively looked away. In that moment, memories of her childhood flashed in my mind. That crinkle in the corner of her eyes when she would smile, her contagious smile. But just as quickly as the memory popped in my mind, it was gone. It left me facing the stark reality of her present situation right there in front of me.

I was overwhelmed again. The woman sitting twenty feet in front of me with a bailiff at her side was my sister, but it didn't seem like the sister I had known. She was a stranger. The difference between the vibrant Angelee I knew and the hollow one in front of me was glaringly obvious; it was just all too much. Guilt, shame and horror washed over me all at once. I felt lightheaded and unable to process the enormity of what I was witnessing.

"All rise," a voice commanded, shaking me from my thoughts.

Everyone in the room stood as the judge entered and took his seat at the bench. I wonder what my son saw on my face when I glanced over at him. I'm sure we shared expressions of fear as we both slowly shook our heads in acknowledgment of the scene in front of us. We focused our attention forward as the judge started to outline how the proceedings were going to go.

I couldn't shake the heavy sense of guilt that was rising in me. How did we get here? I failed her, or at least that's how it felt. Knowing what she had done and seeing her here like this had me wrestling with a variety of emotions. There was still a growing anger for what she had done. The sadness for what she had lost. Then there was the shame I felt for the part I played, or rather didn't play, in her life. Everything was settling deeper and churning in my gut.

The judge was speaking, but I was stuck staring at the back of Angelee's head. I just couldn't shake the thoughts of her as a kid. The memories of her running around the living room at Grandma's. How she could light up an entire room with that laugh. They kept spinning through my mind, one right after another. Those memories used to be a source of comfort that now only deepened the tragedy in front of me. That little girl had vanished, leaving this woman I could hardly recognize. The past was gone and I was left here in this courtroom to face the harshness of the present.

Although the steadying force of my son was reassuring, the guilt of exposing him to this was constantly getting heavier. The worst was still to come. I kept thinking about the look Angelee gave me in that quick moment of eye contact. What was she feeling? Why couldn't I maintain eye contact? There was no escaping what was about to unfold. This was only the beginning of a very long journey, and I didn't know how much more I was truly able to take.

CHAPTER 18: MY CURRENT MINDSET

As I'm writing this and the events that are about to be divulged, I'd like to take pause. I'm really trying to share my experience as honestly and intimately as possible. I believe there's value in bearing witness to these events just as I did and with the same amount of limited knowledge and emotional uncertainty. It's about sharing those raw emotions—the confusion, the helplessness, and the overwhelming dread of what was about to be revealed. To express what those weights felt like, and to better understand how moments like these have the power to reshape everything you thought you knew.

By doing so, I feel it's the most effective way to convey the deeper truth, one that became crystal clear to me: the absolute importance of mental health in today's world. What unfolded in that courtroom, for me, was not just about what happened, but it was also about the fragility of the mind, and how when it's broken, it can lead to the unimaginable. I hope by sharing my experience, it will shed some light on just how critical it is to understand and address mental health. Not just in Angelee's case, but for society as a whole.

When I first heard that Angelee was pleading not guilty by reason of insanity, I was in complete shock. It didn't make any sense at all. My knee-jerk reaction was that this was some kind of legal strategy, something her defense had come up with to minimize her sentence. There was just absolutely no way that she was insane. My little sister had always been strong, determined and resilient. How is it even possible that suddenly, she wasn't capable of knowing right from wrong? No. It doesn't fit. The skeptic inside me felt it was more like a ploy than a truth.

For months leading up to the hearing, I just kept circling back to that same thought. There's absolutely no way that Angelee is actually insane. I was convincing myself that whatever evidence these experts produced would somehow prove she was just finding a way to avoid the consequences of her actions, that it wasn't a mental health issue. This had to be the case; it was the only thing that could make sense.

As the hearing approached, even as I sat in the gallery itself, I kept grappling with it. On one hand, I was trying to push down the idea that the plea was a complete sham. On the other hand, I was clinging to the hope that something during this whole thing would make sense by explaining something that I had yet to consider. Linearly and logically, things must add up to be reasonable in my mind.

Having this skepticism created an underlying tension that had shaped my entire emotional state leading up to this point. I just didn't trust the plea, it didn't line up with anything I could reconcile with her. Then there was the way that I couldn't voice these doubts without feeling even more guilty for questioning her. Nothing made sense, my emotional state was a wreck, and I had no idea what to expect. I just hoped I'd been missing some critical information, a denominator that would have helped in understanding.

So… once the testimonies began, everything shifted.

Hearing those firsthand accounts from the folks who had interacted with her during those times—that's when the bomb dropped. Their descriptions of her behavior. The chaotic spiral she had been in. The clear and obvious struggles she was having with her mental health. This was not just a legal tactic, and for the first time, I realized Angelee had truly been lost, consumed by a mental illness so severe that it had taken over her life. This was not the person I knew, not during this period in her life. It was someone whose mind had betrayed her in ways I could never have imagined.

As I came to terms with this realization, my emotions began to shift yet again. I had been determined to believe this wasn't real, but those testimonies forced me to confront the truth, and it was heartbreaking. Everything I thought I understood was turned upside down, my sister had been taken over by something completely out of her control. I was so conflicted and felt even more guilty for my earlier skepticism. She had been consumed by her illness.

I hope to paint a clearer picture by sharing these raw and unfiltered emotions and truths. It shows exactly how impossible it was to reconcile the sister I once knew with the person being portrayed in that courtroom. Confusion and doubt filled me. I desperately sought to understand that sometimes mental illness can consume even the strongest people.

What follows will not be easy to read, there's no avoiding that. The details are deeply painful, and I tried not to hold back. Like I said, I wanted to take you on this walk with me, to see these events through my eyes as I learned them. These are the testimonies from those directly involved with the crime and the time immediately afterwards. Told through my point of view as I heard them, as I experienced them, and mostly, as I felt them. I'm hoping that through my words, you'll be able to witness the horror, the profound sadness, and the overwhelming emotions the smothered me, my son, and Bill's friends and family as we learned the devastating events that happened on that fateful night.

CHAPTER 19: BUCKLE UP

The realness of the situation sank in quickly when the judge began to speak. There was a lot he was saying that seemed like routine formalities, and none of it stuck with me. Nothing except the words "People versus Angelee Ross." I sank further into my seat as I stared at the back of my sister's head. I couldn't keep my focus on what he was saying, I felt lost in a fog of confusion.

The first witness the prosecution called was a young lady. She walked nervously to the witness stand and slowly sat as she looked around the room. She raised her hand and took her oath, her voice quiet and timid as she spoke. You could hear the slight tremor in her words. She was visibly shaken as she began telling us about that morning. The feeling of unease was rising within me as I just knew she was going to be unveiling the first truth of many to come.

She told of what started as a seemingly ordinary day, one that quickly spiraled into a nightmare. She left home and was headed to the post office before school to either drop off a package or pick up the mail, I can't remember the exact reason. When she was walking out of the post office to leave, she saw a dark green vehicle that had parked right by her car. It was parked in a way that wouldn't allow her to leave the lot.

She was asked if she recognized the woman in the green car, the one that had blocked her in that morning. She only hesitated for a moment before starting to raise her hand. As she pointed at Angelee, the breath was sucked out of my body. Time slowed down. All I could see was her finger, stretched out and pointing directly at my sister. We all knew it was coming, but seeing it and hearing her say, "She's right there" was something I wasn't ever ready for. Angelee sat there motionlessly as the young lady confirmed what we had anticipated. It was Angelee.

The young lady got back into her car. With Angelee blocking her in, she had to carefully maneuver her car as she backed up, so as not to collide with her. When she pulled out of the parking lot, Angelee followed her closely. The young lady started to get scared and drove straight home. She pulled into her driveway, and for some unknown reason, Angelee pulled into her driveway as well and parked right behind her. A new sense of urgency rose within her as she noticed Angelee get out of her vehicle and approach her passenger-side window.

In a haste, she tried to push the button to ensure her doors were locked but accidentally hit the window button. It lowered the passenger-side window ever so slightly. That's when she was able to see the full scope of what was happening. Angelee stood at the passenger door, completely naked and covered from head to toe in something like dried mud. The sight was both shocking and terrifying for her. Despite her fear, the young lady was able to ensure the doors were locked.

Angelee carried an unnerving calm about her as she stood there, repeatedly asking if she could get in. Her voice was composed yet detached, which varied greatly from the panic that was growing inside the vehicle. Realizing the severity of the situation and being overcome with fear, the young lady called her mother who was inside the house. She hurriedly explained to her mom what was happening just outside their front door, begging her to come outside and help. There was no mistaking the terror in her voice, and the more she spoke, the worse it became.

When her mom came out, or possibly just looked out the front window, Angelee hurried back to her car. Even though she was hurrying, it was with a strange, eerie calm. Without any missed steps, Angelee got into her vehicle, turned, and drove straight across the young lady's lawn. She was visibly shaken as she summed up Angelee's bizarre behavior with a single word: weird.

I was engulfed in disbelief. My thoughts were persistent. How in the world is this person that she's describing, my sister? It just didn't add up. The picture of Angelee I had in my mind was of the modest and caring person who would never scare anyone on purpose. This picture was being shattered by the young lady's testimony. Angelee was driving around naked, covered in something, scaring people. I couldn't wrap my head around it. The baseline of who Angelee was and what I was hearing just didn't align.

I knew Angelee had battled depression most of her life, and that it was accompanied with extreme, manic mood swings. There were plenty of highs and lows. But this was way beyond any of that. Had I misunderstood the seriousness of her condition? I could confront that truth, but explaining this was something else altogether.

I was expecting something less shocking. Something that may have stretched the boundaries of what I knew but would still fit within the framework of the person I was familiar with. What I was hearing instead were these actions that were completely foreign to her character. At this point, I wasn't really questioning who she was, I was wondering what had happened to her to make this happen. I hadn't seen her in quite some time, and we all change over time, but this just felt too extreme. It was too far removed from anything I had ever experienced in real life.

It was still too early to make any sense of it. I felt as though we hadn't even scratched the surface of truth. We were already being exposed to unimaginable things, how could it possibly get any worse?

CHAPTER 20: A CRASH, TYVEK AND BOMBSHELLS

An elderly gentleman was the next person to take the stand. His calm and measured demeanor showed little emotion as he approached. Still, there was something about the way he carried himself, something that spoke of the burden he bore from those events. The vibe in the courtroom was tense as he started his testimony. He wasn't just describing any other day, he was about to tell the story of a deeply unsettling morning that left a mark on all those involved.

He told the story of having picked up his grandchildren just after seven a.m. They were teenagers, and he was bringing them back home to his house. It was one of those routines that usually fades into the background of your day. When he got a bit closer to his house, something caught his attention. There was a green Tahoe parked on the wrong side of the street, facing the wrong direction. Nothing to really raise a red flag, but odd enough to notice. But then, as he passed, it pulled out and started to follow him; that was odd. He continued on his way.

He made the last turn onto his street and realized the Tahoe was turning as well, still following him. He pulled into the driveway of his home, put the car in park, and turned to say something to his grandkids. That's when his anxiety started to spike. Through the back window, he saw that same green Tahoe pulling into his driveway as well—and accelerating fast. The Tahoe slammed into the back of his car with such a jarring impact that it shoved his own car forward a few feet.

In a fit of anger, he jumped out of the car and started heading towards the Tahoe ready to confront the intruder. What he saw through the windshield of the offending vehicle was a woman in the driver's seat—a naked woman.

It must have been the sound of the crash that drew his wife's attention because at this moment, she walked out of the house. Still fuming, the man turned to his wife and told her she needed to deal with this since the woman didn't have any clothes on. His wife started to talk with Angelee, who was awake and seemingly aware. But her expression, or rather absence of one, was what really struck them as odd. The man's wife tried to ask her who she was and if she was ok. But Angelee just sat there looking at her, or more correctly, looking straight through his wife. He mentioned that she had a spaced-out look to her, like someone who had been on narcotics.

The elderly gentleman retreated to his house to grab something, anything to cover Angelee with to allow her some sort of dignity during this strange incident. They began to believe she may have been a victim of something at this point and started treating her as such. She was completely covered in dried blood. He found a one-piece chemical suit like the Tyvek painters use.

They called 911 right away, realizing something was truly amiss there and that they needed help to handle it. As they waited, they managed to coax the overalls onto Angelee's blood-stained body. When they were finally able to get the suit on as much as they could manage, she just slumped over, right over the middle console and into the passenger seat.

As the older gentleman finished up his testimony, I was thinking, What the hell? Trying to absorb everything I had just heard was heavy and painful. That pit that was in my stomach was not just a vague feeling—it physically hurt me. My hands were trembling, my chest was tight. I was frozen in my seat, trapped in a nightmare I couldn't wake up from. The pieces of what I was hearing just didn't fit together. It was like trying to complete a puzzle with pieces from three different boxes.

He passed right in front of me as he walked out of the courtroom, but I couldn't even really see him. I found myself staring at the back of Angelee's head again, just looking for some familiar sign, something I could recognize. Whatever was going on with her, it was going far deeper than I had ever imagined. I started to recognize a pattern: each testimony was going to leave me with so many more questions than answers.

CHAPTER 21: FIRST RESPONDER'S TESTIMONY

A seasoned lieutenant for the local volunteer fire department had been dispatched to the accident. He was the next person to take the stand. He was the first professional to speak about what happened, and the shift in the courtroom was noticeable. As the firefighter approached the stand, there was a different weight to his presence. The uniform he wore, his calm demeanor, and his ability to hold a steady gaze all spoke to his ability and experience in handling emergencies. But still, there was something about him. Maybe it was the way he sat down and gave a quick glance in Angelee's direction. Maybe it was something else, but something hinted that the call he was about to detail was not a routine call. Whatever he was about to share, I was nervous to hear.

The lieutenant spoke with an authoritative voice that was steady and sure, probably from years of carrying memories too heavy to forget. His words were measured, but it was obvious that what he had witnessed that morning had left an impact.

He Described walking up to the vehicles and saw Angelee slumped over the steering wheel. She appeared to be fading in and out. He noticed her wrist on the gear shifter, the car still running. She was covered in blood, which didn't fit the scene he was currently standing in. There were no shattered windows, no air bags had been deployed. This was not fresh blood from a traffic accident; this was dried blood, and copious amounts of it that covered her entire body, even her hair. It clung to her like a second skin.

He stood there momentarily, trying to absorb exactly what he was seeing. He walked around to the passenger side and opened the door, he knew he needed to turn the vehicle off and take the keys, just in case. He called out to her and tapped her on the shoulder, she looked up immediately. He started asking her routine questions. What's your name? Date of birth? Where are you? Those questions turned up mixed results. Her voice was distant, as if she was somewhere else mentally. She did give him her name, kind of answered her birthday, and only had a rough idea of where she was.

Then there was the answer to the question of what happened that left him shellshocked. Angelee's response was so simplistic and so alarming. She just kept repeating that she wanted help, that she needed help and was trying to get away. Her voice remained toneless, soft and broken. Those same words, over and over, spoken with raw desperation. Then, out of nowhere, she said, "I killed Bill" and provided him the address of where it happened. He kept her talking, trying to keep her focused because she said she felt herself slipping away.

Gently, he pressed further about Bill. The words that came from her next sent an audible gasp from somewhere in the gallery of the courtroom. She told him that she had beat him until he stopped moving, had stabbed him, and done more. It must have felt surreal for lieutenant because as soon as those words left her mouth, she chuckled.

An odd, almost relieved laugh, maybe with a hint of madness. The sound, he admitted, still echoed in his mind like a bad dream.

I was beside myself with confusion. Wait, what?! Her laugh? Angelee's laugh had always been so full of life, so genuine. It was loud and obnoxious but loving. How could it ever sound like anything else? The image of Angelee telling such a brutal story with that strange laugh at the end was beyond deeply unsettling. I couldn't even move, terrified of what else might be revealed about that night.

Realizing the gravity of the situation, the lieutenant immediately requested not only a welfare check at the address she gave him, but also the immediate presence of the Michigan State Police at his location for Angelee. Her confession hung in the air, thick and constricting.

The defense attorney had one item of clarification for him. She asked him to clarify what he meant when he said Angelee was "in and out." Was she drifting in and out of consciousness? He shook his head no, explaining it wasn't exactly consciousness, it was more like extreme exhaustion. He described Angelee as she kept trying to rest her head on the steering wheel, like she was too tired to stay awake. The defense attorney pressed a little further, asking for his impression of her mental state. His response was immediate. She seemed like someone desperately seeking help and needing it immediately.

CHAPTER 22:
THE AMBULANCE RIDE

The last two witnesses to testify that morning were Laura and Stan, the EMT and paramedic, each offering their accounts of interacting with Angelee. One by one, they took the stand. Their testimonies only deepened the suffocating tension in the courtroom, each sentence pulling us further into the unfolding nightmare. Those of us in the gallery remained frozen in our seats, as if afraid that even the smallest movement might break the fragile stillness. There was a noticeable, hushed anticipation—not of excitement, but of deep, shared apprehension. Each testimony seemed to pull loose another thread of the unraveling story, and with every new detail, the darkness grew deeper, more haunting, and more impossible to ignore.

Laura was the first to take the stand. She was calm yet resolute. She began her testimony by explaining how she arrived at the scene and immediately assessed the situation. She described how she first approached the group of people standing near the garage. Her job was to triage those in the elderly man's car.

Laura mentioned that the vehicles were damaged but not totaled. It had all the makings of a routine accident at first glance. She conducted her initial assessment of the elderly man and his passengers, checking for any visible injuries. She noted that, thankfully, there appeared to be no immediate need for transport to the hospital.

Their vitals were stable, and aside from the shock of the collision, none of the passengers displayed signs of life-threatening injuries. It was clear from her tone that she had expected this to be just another unfortunate but typical accident.

But then, everything changed.

She turned toward her partner, Stan, who was walking toward her from the other vehicle, his expression portraying a subtle urgency. Instinctively, she knew something was off—something far more serious than what they had initially assumed. She was likely expecting him to share an update about the condition of the woman in the green Tahoe, perhaps believing that her injuries were more severe than they'd first realized. But nothing could have prepared her for the revelation that was about to come.

Stan began recounting what Angelee had said, delivering the shocking details like a bombshell. The gravity of his words seemed to hang in the air, too heavy to fully sink in at that moment. But as they approached the Tahoe to move Angelee to the ambulance, reality closed in around Laura. That's when she saw Angelee—covered in blood. The sight of her must have sent a shockwave through Laura, as she recalled how they loaded Angelee into the ambulance. The thick layer of dried blood surely felt surreal beneath Laura's gloved hands.

Inside the ambulance, something shifted for Laura. What had always been a controlled, sterile environment—a place of calm amidst chaos—now felt different. The bright, fluorescent lights overhead illuminated just how much blood was on Angelee. Her long hair was matted and stiff and had become one large, tangled mass crusted with dried blood. As Angelee spoke, her voice soft yet filled with an unsettling mix of awareness and confusion, Laura realized that this was no ordinary scene. This was something far more disturbing.

The rumble of the ambulance engine became the backdrop to a strange and disjointed conversation. As they drove toward the hospital, Stan questioned Angelee about her condition, asking the routine inquiries. Her responses were fragmented, inconsistent, and erratic, as though she was struggling to string together coherent thoughts. Laura noted that, beneath Angelee's soft voice, there was an underlying sense of suspense, an unease that hinted at something much deeper. It was becoming more and more evident that something was profoundly wrong.

Amidst her jumbled speech, Angelee kept repeating a chilling phrase over and over again: "I killed him. I killed him." Each time the words left her mouth, they seemed to echo off the walls of the ambulance, reverberating through the small space. Laura recalled how those words filled the air, suffocating the atmosphere, making the already cramped ambulance feel even smaller. I could feel myself shaking my head, desperately trying to deny what I was hearing. No, this couldn't be true. It was beyond comprehension. How could this be happening?

Then, in a sudden, surreal twist, Angelee's words shifted to "I killed him. I killed him. Can you take me to Florida?" Florida? What? The abrupt change in her dialogue only added another layer of confusion to an already incomprehensible situation. One moment, she was confessing to the most unimaginable act, and the next, she was asking to go to Florida, as if nothing had happened. Stan and Laura exchanged a quick glance through the mirror, but they didn't press her further.

When they finally arrived at the hospital, Angelee thanked Laura and Stan for "doing God's work." It was a bizarre statement, delivered with such sincerity that it left Laura momentarily speechless. She knew something was horribly wrong with Angelee, but exactly what was beyond her comprehension. It was unlike anything she had ever encountered in her career.

When Stan took the stand, he brought even more depth to the already complex situation. His tone was steady and measured as he recounted how Angelee's thoughts jumped from one topic to another without any clear connection between them, as if she were caught in an endless loop of confusion. She was alert and fully conscious, but her mind was far from clear. She was trapped in a delusional state, unable to make sense of the reality around her.

He also described Angelee's physical state, noting how the crusted blood on her face didn't align with typical car accident injuries, especially at the speed they estimated. It wasn't from an impact, but looked rather like a spray pattern, the kind associated with trauma from close-range violence. The sight of the blood, splattered in a way that defied explanation, seemed to freeze the air around him. He had seen countless blood patterns in his line of work, but this one was different. It wasn't from a typical crash.

Throughout the ride to the hospital, Angelee continued to speak freely, her words a mix of random, scattered thoughts and confessions. She spoke about doing the right thing, about fulfilling some higher purpose, convinced that she was carrying out a divine mission. Stan explained how he made the conscious decision not to challenge her delusions, knowing how fragile her mental state was. Instead, he let her talk, hoping to keep the situation calm and under control.

As I sat there listening to the testimonies, the enormity of it all settled like a cold knot in my chest. The details were more than just unnerving—they were terrifying. They offered a glimpse into the shattered state of Angelee's mind, revealing a world where reality had blurred beyond recognition. What we saw through that window was a mind unraveling, crossing the line between confusion and something far darker. I wish I could find the words to describe the emotions that filled me in that moment, but they felt almost too heavy to put to words properly. It was as if the weight of the truth was pressing down on all of us, and we were powerless to stop it.

CHAPTER 23: BEARING THE BURDEN

The judge announced a forty-five-minute recess for lunch, offering us a brief chance to step away from the intensity of the courtroom. No one moved at first, as if the gravity of the morning's proceedings had left us all stuck in place, overwhelmed by what we had just witnessed. I watched as the bailiff approached Angelee, gently helping her to her feet. She stood without resistance, not looking back, her head hanging low like the weight of the moment was too much for her to carry alone.

My son and I, seated closest to the door, were the first to rise. We quickly left the courtroom, trying to escape the suffocating tension that clung to the air. There was a silence between us that was heavy with unspoken thoughts. It felt as though any words might shatter the fragile calm. As we stepped outside, the bright sunlight hit our faces with a force that felt almost cruel. It was a beautiful spring day, one that should have brought peace, but instead seemed mocking, presenting everything as normal when, in reality, nothing was.

We hurried to the car and sat in silence. The stillness around us was conflicting, both calming and suffocating. I was exhausted, and the relentless sunlight poured into the car through the windshield, only adding to my discomfort. The chill from the morning still lingered in the air. As I sat there, I realized my jaw was clenched and my hands were gripping the steering wheel, even though we weren't going anywhere. The tension in my chest made it hard to breathe, and I stared ahead, my mind a blur, weighed down by confusion and helplessness.

I don't know how long we sat there, lost in our own thoughts. It could have been minutes or hours. Finally, I broke the silence. "Are you hungry?" I asked my son, my voice sounding foreign, as though I hadn't spoken in days. He shook his head slightly, admitting he wasn't. We knew we couldn't just sit in the parking lot; too many chance encounters were possible, and we needed a distraction. Eating felt pointless, but it was something to do.

Unfamiliar with the area, I drove toward the outskirts of town. For a fleeting moment, I considered to just keep going, to drive home and leave all of this behind. But I knew that wasn't an option. We ended up pulling into an old A&W restaurant, though I'm not sure why. Maybe because it looked familiar, like a place we had been to a hundred times before, even though we hadn't. Inside, it was nearly empty, the decor outdated. The sun streamed through the windows, harsh and unforgiving, making it impossible to ignore how worn down we both were. I couldn't help but wish for a gloomy, overcast day to better match the weight of our emotions.

The smell of fried food hung heavy in the air, normally comforting but now nauseating. We ordered something, neither of us caring what it was. The food arrived quickly, but it was tasteless, and we ate mechanically, barely aware of what we were doing. I was grateful for my son's presence; otherwise, I might have just sat there, lost in thought, too afraid to return. We spoke a little, but every conversation circled back to trying and failing to make sense of what we had heard.

But none of it made sense. Nothing about this felt real, and the hardest part was knowing that there was still more to come.

When we returned to the courthouse parking lot, we saw Bill's friends and family gathered outside again. My chest tightened at the sight of them, guilt and shame flooding over me. Normally, I was good in difficult situations. I'd be able to step in, offer comfort, find the right words. This was different. It was personal, and for the first time in my life, I had no idea what to say.

I wanted to approach them, to express how sorry I was for their pain. But I knew my words weren't welcome. My throat tightened, and the shame weighed me down. How could I offer comfort when my own sister had caused their suffering? The words I wanted to say were beyond my reach, just as the courage to face them was. I felt like a bystander, helpless in a situation that demanded more, but I had nothing to give.

We silently walked back inside, the weight of the afternoon ahead pressing down on us. Knowing that nothing I could say or do would make this right was a heavy burden, one that I would carry with me long after the hearing was over.

CHAPTER 24: SIGNALS OF DISTRESS

During their investigation, the Michigan State Police meticulously pieced together information from various sources, one of the most revealing being Bill's boss at the auto parts store where Bill had worked for over three years. As the trooper testified about the interview with Bill's boss, a crucial perspective was provided that shed light on the days leading up to the tragedy, which offered context to help make sense of what had happened. Although this account isn't verbatim, it accurately captures the facts as I recall them, paraphrased here:

Bill was widely known for his unwavering dedication and commitment to his job. He had earned a reputation as a model employee—someone you could count on. Whether it was arriving early to cover a shift or stepping in when things got busy, Bill was always reliable. His strong work ethic stood out, making him the type of person who rarely, if ever, deviated from his routine. This steadfastness is what made the events leading up to that fateful day all the more perplexing.

In his conversation with the police, Bill's boss spoke highly of him, recalling how rare it was for Bill to call out of work or act in any way that would suggest something was wrong. So when Bill shared some troubling details about Angelee's behavior in the days before the incident, it was clear that something unusual was unfolding. Bill confided that Angelee had begun displaying increasingly bizarre and erratic behavior at home. She had removed all the smoke detectors from their home, unplugged the microwave, and disconnected any other appliances that were still plugged in. Bill explained to his boss that Angelee believed they were being watched, that people were listening in on them through these devices.

But it didn't stop there. Bill told his boss that Angelee had started talking about a space shuttle, claiming it was on its way. The shuttle was part of some delusional narrative that had seemed to grip her. The most alarming detail was her insistence that "the purge" was real and that it wasn't some distant possibility—it was happening right then. The gravity of this confession wasn't lost on Bill, who seemed deeply concerned but still determined to take care of her and get her the help she needed.

It was sometime after 5:30 a.m. when Bill left his boss an uncharacteristically cryptic voicemail. He explained that he wouldn't be coming to work that day due to personal issues involving Angelee. This voicemail was unlike anything Bill had ever left before—he never missed work, and he certainly never called in for personal issues. Bill also mentioned in the message that the power had gone out at his house. There was a noticeable sense of concern in his voice, and while the message was brief, it suggested that something serious was happening at home. It was clear that things were spiraling beyond Bill's control.

PART III
AT THE HOSPITAL

CHAPTER 25:
WHISPERS OF MADNESS

When the EMT and paramedic dropped Angelee off at the emergency room, the strangeness didn't just persist—it intensified. From the moment she arrived, it became glaringly clear to the hospital staff that something was deeply wrong. It wasn't just her physical state but the unsettling aura surrounding her. The staff immediately knew they were in over their heads and realized they would need assistance from the police.

The emergency room, usually a place of controlled chaos, now felt on the verge of slipping out of control. The familiar hustle of scrub-clad nurses and doctors moving swiftly, the sharp scent of antiseptic, the steady beeping of machines remained, but the atmosphere had shifted. Curtains scraped on metal rings, the harsh sound punctuating the unsettling stillness that had taken hold of the room. What began as a normal morning was now drenched in an eerie air, as if the room itself was struggling to contain a situation spiraling out of their control.

Angelee was restless, unable to stay in the hospital bed for more than a few moments. No amount of coaxing could keep her contained. She kept ripping off her hospital gown, wandering around the emergency room naked without a care. The staff, accustomed to crises of all kinds, were caught off guard. Other patients looked on in shock and were equally disturbed by the erratic behavior unfolding before them. Angelee's actions defied logic, her words made no sense, and there was no clear connection between what she said and what she did. They quickly moved her to a private room behind the nurses' station, hoping the police would arrive soon. It was clear that Angelee was utterly disconnected from reality, lost in her own chaotic world.

Trooper Hawthorne, the first to arrive, had been working a case at the prison when the call came in. Though he had dealt with strange situations before, nothing could have prepared him for what he saw. When he first laid eyes on Angelee, he was stunned. Despite his years of experience, this was unlike anything he had encountered. She sat completely naked in a small room near the nurses' station, utterly indifferent to her surroundings. Her entire body was covered in blood that was flaking and crusted. Even her hands, down to the cuticles, were caked with blood so deeply embedded it seemed almost fused to her. The way Hawthorne described it was chilling, as if she had been encased in a shell of blood, like something out of a nightmare.

But it wasn't her appearance that unnerved him the most—it was her voice. Angelee spoke with terrifying clarity, her words sharp and disturbingly calm. The disconnect between her disheveled appearance and the articulate way she spoke was almost surreal. She wasn't ranting or raving, as he might have expected. Instead, she was composed—eerily composed—as though nothing was amiss. Then, without hesitation, she locked eyes with Hawthorne and simply said, "I murdered my friend." It wasn't an emotional confession. There was no regret, no panic—just a statement of fact. The horror of what she had done hadn't fully registered with her. Realizing how lucid she seemed, Hawthorne immediately knew he needed to Mirandize her.

As he read her rights, Hawthorne felt the weight of every word. The usual routine of reciting rights felt heavier, burdened by the enormity of the situation. He read each right slowly, ensuring she understood, and she nodded after each with no hesitation, eager to keep talking. It felt as though she had been waiting for someone to listen, as if this was her moment to unload.

Her words, however, were anything but coherent. What followed was a scattered whirlwind of religious references and fragmented memories that didn't fit together. She leaped from one topic to the next with no logical flow, her thoughts racing too quickly to form a complete picture. Hawthorne tried to guide her gently, hoping to piece together a timeline, but it was futile. She mentioned God several times, describing herself as a child of God and insisting that God was on her side. There was something profoundly discomforting about the way she spoke—detached, almost euphoric, like she had transcended the reality of what had happened.

At one point, Angelee's story shifted to her relationship with Bill. She described how they had been living together as boyfriend and girlfriend, claiming he used her for sex and to clean the house. It wasn't what she said that disturbed Hawthorne, it was how she said it. Her tone was cold and unemotional, and she talked about the situation like she was merely reciting a list of facts. When Hawthorne asked how things had escalated to violence, her response was chilling. "I killed Bill. His soul needed to be cleansed. He's a bad person." Again, her response was flat and disassociated from the act in her confession.

Hawthorne pressed further, asking if she had been using any drugs. Perhaps that could explain her behavior. Angelee didn't miss a beat, admitting to using methamphetamine. For the first time in their conversation, Hawthorne noticed a flicker of emotion—frustration. She expressed regret not for killing Bill, but for having disgraced her body, her "temple," with drugs. The idea of tainting herself with meth apparently weighed more heavily on her than the murder she had committed.

Her narrative continued to unfold. It was a jumbled mess of disjointed thoughts and splintered memories. She spoke of seeing "lights" and described, in detail, the gun locker Bill had kept in the house. She was fixated on the lock, though Hawthorne struggled to see its relevance. At one point, she mentioned Bill calling her a bitch during an argument. When Hawthorne asked if this argument had sparked the violence, she denied any connection. Then, bizarrely, she claimed Bill would often hand her a gun during their arguments. Hawthorne could hardly believe what he was hearing. He shook his head, trying to make sense of her words. Why would Bill trust her with a gun during an argument? But she insisted it was true, and that it was a regular occurrence.

Angelee's story then turned to the murder itself. She described how she found herself holding a gun and, in that moment, realized Bill's soul needed cleansing. She pulled the trigger. Initially, she thought she had hit him in the chest, but she wasn't sure. She remembered kicking him down the stairs, watching his body tumble. Then, somehow, a lamp was in her hands. She didn't know where it came from, but she used it to strike Bill repeatedly in the head until the lamp broke. And then there was a knife. She couldn't recall how she got it, but she used it to stab him—maybe in the heart, maybe in the chest. The details were blurry.

Hawthorne stood there, reeling from the horrific words spilling from her mouth. He asked if she thought the gunshot had been what killed Bill. Angelee quickly responded, "No." She was certain Bill had still been alive when she started beating him. In fact, she claimed he had punched her in the head during the attack. The details were muddled, but one thing was clear: she had killed him. And her reason? "I did it for me. I did it to prove to God I am worthy." The words, hollow and devoid of emotion, chilled Hawthorne to his core.

Suddenly, as if drained of all energy, Angelee lay back in the hospital bed. She closed her eyes and appeared to drift off to sleep, her body finally still. The weight of her confession pressed down on Hawthorne like a suffocating cloud. The calmness with which she had recounted the brutally violent acts starkly contrasted the horror of what she had done. It was almost impossible to reconcile. How could someone so serene, so composed be capable of such unimaginable violence?

As the trooper continued his report, I felt as though the ground beneath me was giving way. How could my sister—the person I love, the person I thought I knew—be capable of such horrors? I sat there numb, my mind refusing to fully accept the truth that had just been laid before me.

CHAPTER 26:
BLOOD-STAINED REALITIES

As Trooper Hawthorne stood watch over Angelee, he described how she began to make more unsolicited statements, almost as if she were having a conversation with herself. Perhaps she was trying to make sense of the chaos in her mind. Her soft, hauntingly distant voice echoed through the room. "God loves me. I'll be forgiven," she'd say, clinging to the words as if seeking some form of comfort. "I want to be pain-free with God." Her voice remained steady, disturbingly so, as if this belief would somehow absolve her of everything that had happened. But these weren't just simple statements, they were fragments from a mind that had been shattered, a consciousness desperately grasping for something to hold on to, no matter how twisted or distorted that reality was.

Despite his years of experience handling difficult and unpredictable situations, this was unsettling, unfamiliar territory for Trooper Hawthorne. The disconnect between her words and the vicious reality of what had taken place left him searching for some coherent thread. He asked probing questions, hoping to get a clearer narrative, but her responses remained scattered and broken.

Like leaves tossed about in the wind, her words drifted aimlessly and landed without purpose.

When he asked if Bill had used drugs as well, hoping for something that might make sense of it all, Angelee admitted she had given him meth once. He pressed further, asking if Bill had smoked or injected it, and her answers remained vague and elusive. The conversation was like trying to grasp smoke.

In an effort to keep the conversation going, he asked if she had harmed anyone else. He wasn't expecting much, but her response froze him. Her face took on a frighteningly serene expression as she calmly stated, "I killed Bill's dogs as well." The words, delivered in the same matter-of-fact tone as everything else, sent a chill down Trooper Hawthorne's spine. He pressed for more details, trying to understand, but her answers offered no clarity.

Angelee wasn't sure exactly how she had killed them, only that "they needed to be sent to heaven." She said she knew they were dead because "they weren't moving anymore." She spoke of it as if it were the most ordinary thing in the world, and it was deeply unnerving. Hawthorne later described the interaction as "just very, very strange," though this barely scratched the surface of the horror and confusion he felt while trying to process her confessions.

During this surreal interaction, Hawthorne's phone rang. The call was from his sergeant. Unable to leave Angelee unattended, he stepped towards the far wall to take the call. His sergeant asked if, based on what he had gathered, this could possibly be a case of self-defense. Without thinking about the possibility of Angelee overhearing him, Hawthorne quickly replied that he did not believe it was self-defense. Immediately, Angelee sat up in bed and interrupted, "Yes. Yes, it was self-defense." Trying to maintain his composure, Hawthorne turned away from her and reiterated to his sergeant that he did not think self-defense was the case. When he ended the call and turned back to face her, she spoke again, contradicting herself. "It was not self-defense. I killed him. His soul needed to be cleaned. I am not a victim." Hawthorne's voice wavered as he recounted this moment—how disturbing her shifting narrative was, and how she seemed to try on different versions of the truth, unable or unwilling to commit to any of them. She seemed to be trapped in a maze of her own mind, lost and unable to find a way out.

Trooper Hawthorne cautiously described her overall demeanor as "crazy," a word he used sparingly but felt was appropriate here. He had witnessed countless homicides over his career, but nothing had prepared him for this. Her complete disconnection from the reality of her actions was unlike anything he had encountered before. At one point in the courtroom, he even looked at her and, with a touch of disbelief, said, "No offense, ma'am, but just absolutely crazy" when asked to describe her state of detachment.

One image Hawthorne kept returning to again and again was that of her blood-stained hands. The blood was packed so tightly into her cuticles that it reminded him of someone who had spent an entire day digging in bare earth with their hands. The sight of those blood-stained hands would linger in his mind long after he left that room.

Hawthorne was alone with Angelee for quite some time as they waited for the female officer he had requested. During this period, her erratic behavior resurfaced. She couldn't stay still, was constantly standing up and walking around, and repeatedly stripped off her hospital gown. She seemed to prefer being naked, and as time passed, she began to fixate on Hawthorne, particularly staring at his genital area. And she made no effort to hide it. Feeling increasingly uncomfortable, Hawthorne moved closer to the door, which he had intentionally kept cracked open. He needed to ensure there was no absolute privacy between them. But Angelee repeatedly walked over and attempted to close the door, another sign that she had no understanding of boundaries, no comprehension of the inappropriateness of her actions.

Hawthorne's time with her was surreal, unsettling, and profoundly disturbing. It was clear that Angelee was lost in a world of her own, disconnected from the reality of what she had done and incapable of grasping the gravity of her situation. As Trooper Hawthorne stood watch, he realized that the horror of her confessions was only one layer of the twisted, chaotic mind unraveling before him.

CHAPTER 27: INSIDE THE STORM

Trooper Blake was in the middle of another investigation when she was urgently called to assist at the hospital. With years of expertise in drug recognition, she was the obvious choice for the task. Her exceptional ability to detect when someone was under the influence had been honed through years of training and experience. But this wasn't just another routine call; there was an overarching sense of urgency in the dispatcher's voice that set it apart. A woman named Angelee had been involved in a car accident, was now in the emergency room, and had made confessions that held some serious weight.

As Trooper Blake drove towards the hospital, her mind raced through possible scenarios she may encounter—blood, panic, hysteria, the typical responses her experience had conditioned her to expect. However, when she arrived, the scene was nothing like she had anticipated.

Upon entering the emergency room, the staff quickly pointed her towards where she was needed. She saw Trooper Hawthorne standing in the doorway of a room behind the nurses' station. He began briefing her on the situation as she approached, but over his shoulder, Blake caught her first glimpse of Angelee. Naked and caked in blood.

Blake moved closer to Angelee, trying to grasp the full extent of the situation. Without any prompting, Angelee greeted her with a flat, emotionless statement. "I'm not worthy. I'm not worthy." Blake glanced back at Hawthorne, who simply shrugged. In that instant, Blake knew something was profoundly wrong. This wasn't just shock or trauma. Angelee's demeanor, her words, her very presence indicated that she had slipped into a removed, surreal reality.

Blake tried to reassure her by speaking softly and explaining that they were there to help. No matter what she said, Angelee's response remained the same: "I'm not worthy." Each attempt to engage her was met with this unsettling, repetitive loop. Blake tried to make sense of the sporadic words Hawthorne had mentioned earlier, but it was clear that Angelee was stuck in her own emotionless loop, disconnected from the reality of the hospital room and the officers standing in front of her.

A soft knock at the door signaled the arrival of a staff tech, announcing that Angelee's CT scan was ready. They needed to take her down the hall for the procedure. Trooper Hawthorne followed to ensure nothing went awry.

When they returned about ten minutes later, Blake decided it was time to ask the question that had been nagging at her since she arrived. Lowering her voice, she asked Angelee gently if she had taken any drugs or medications. Again, Angelee calmly admitted to taking meth.

Blake's instincts told her that there had to be something in Angelee's system to explain her emotionless state and the clear disconnect from reality. Maybe meth was the simple explanation. Blake asked if she could take a closer look at Angelee. From her years of experience, she knew that women often inject drugs beneath their fingernails, toenails, or between their fingers. But the sheer amount of blood made it difficult to examine. Still, upon closer inspection, she could tell with near certainty that there were no injection marks—certainly none indicating long-term drug use.

Blake then asked Angelee to open her mouth, searching for the signs of tooth decay or gum issues commonly associated with meth users. Again, there were no clear indicators.

Confused, Blake asked Angelee how she had taken the meth. Meeting her gaze with the same eerie collectedness, Angelee responded, "In pill form."

It made some sense, but Blake needed more information. When she asked how long Angelee had been using meth, Angelee's response caught her completely off guard. "I take my Adderall every day." Blake felt her experienced mind racing to process this strange statement. Angelee had nonchalantly swapped meth for Adderall. Was she truly that disconnected from reality? Blake found herself struggling to decipher what was real and what was simply a creation of Angelee's fractured mind.

Blake knew she needed to investigate further. As she inspected Angelee's hands, wrists, and arms, her stomach dropped. Beneath the blood, Blake spotted fresh bruises and swelling, particularly on Angelee's right hand—clear signs of a struggle. A strange puncture wound on Angelee's forearm also caught her attention, making her mentally note it for later. The bruises, cuts, and blood painted a vivid picture of the brutality that had occurred. And yet, Angelee sat there, unnervingly calm, as though nothing had happened.

Blake pressed for more details, and Angelee's responses became increasingly bizarre.

When asked if they needed to check on Bill, both troopers shuddered as Angelee replied, "I killed Bill. He's gone. He's dust."

Angelee's narrative grew stranger with each passing moment. She described seeing red and green lights and hearing the electricity speak to her. Her voice began to shift, becoming almost animated as she relived these surreal visions. She spoke of a powerful surge of energy coursing through her body, something uncontrollable that had driven her to act. Blake stood stunned, listening to Angelee recount these bizarre experiences with growing excitement.

Then, just as quickly as it had appeared, Angelee's excitement faded, and she reverted to the same flat tone she had used earlier. She explained how she had tried to shoot Bill with a gun upstairs, but it had misfired. She felt the energy guide her to push him down the stairs. Angelee then described how she had picked up a lamp and struck Bill repeatedly. In the middle of this recounting, she abruptly changed the subject. "I have to use the restroom. This isn't real anyhow, maybe I should just go right here."

The sudden shift left Blake and Hawthorne momentarily speechless. How could she seamlessly transition from recounting such a terrible act to casually discussing her need for the bathroom? It was becoming evident that Angelee couldn't—or wouldn't—distinguish between two realities. She drifted effortlessly between the two, seemingly unaware of the stark contrast.

Blake tried to redirect the conversation, asking Angelee about Bill's current state.

Angelee's answer were chilling. "He's reincarnated now. Bill wasn't chosen." She went on to explain that the dogs had told her Bill had to die. The dogs, she said, would growl in response to her questions, confirming her belief that she needed to kill him. Each new revelation deepened the unsettling horror of it all.

Leaning back against the wall, Blake tried to make sense of the fragmented, disorienting confession. This wasn't just a typical crime or a drug-fueled incident; it was a descent into madness. Angelee's narrative wasn't grounded in reality, but in a twisted, delusional world she had created for herself. Blake exchanged a glance with Hawthorne, both of them feeling the weight of the incomprehensible story they were unraveling.

Their job wasn't done; they still needed to photograph Angelee to document her injuries.

Despite Angelee's tendency to strip off her gown, Trooper Hawthorne respectfully stepped outside while Blake took the necessary photos. With the door slightly ajar, Hawthorne could still hear if Blake needed assistance. Angelee agreed to the photos without hesitation, and Blake began to carefully document everything.

When Blake asked Angelee to pull her hair back so it wouldn't obstruct the photos, Angelee seemed confused. Blake, wearing latex gloves, gently moved Angelee's hair off her shoulders and adjusted her arms for a clearer view. That's when Blake noticed something disturbing—Angelee was softly moaning. The realization hit hard. Angelee seemed to be enjoying the process. Then, with a sinister smile, she asked Blake, "Where have you been all my life?"

Feeling deeply uncomfortable, Blake quickly called Hawthorne back into the room. This was yet another unsettling first in a day filled with strange, unnerving moments.

As they stood there, grappling with the irrationality of Angelee's behavior, the lead detective, Detective Lockhart, finally arrived. Blake felt a slight sense of relief knowing someone else would now share the burden of untangling this chaotic, disturbing case. One thing was becoming clear: Angelee's warped reality had led her to commit acts as incomprehensible as they were horrific. Piecing it together would be a long, painstaking process.

CHAPTER 28:
THE BLOODBATH

I was still frozen in place, unable to move—afraid to move. The story they were telling, the picture they were painting was unbelievable. I knew I had to believe their words, though. They had to be true. But how? How could the things they were saying, the events they were describing, hold any thread of truth? Yet, I sat there, unable to turn away, listening as Detective Lockhart, recounted the events from the hospital. Like those before him, he had entered that hospital room expecting to see someone shaken, perhaps displaying some remorse or even defiance. But what he encountered was far more unsettling.

Angelee lay in the hospital bed, naked but covered by a blanket. The photographs had been taken just before the detective arrived. She displayed the same calm, detached demeanor others had witnessed. She looked completely unaffected, as if nothing could disturb her peace. Detective Lockhart introduced himself, explained that he needed to conduct an interview, and presented the search warrant for collecting biological samples.

He described Angelee as completely removed from reality. Her vacant gaze along with the serene and casual way she responded to his questions made him wonder if she had any awareness of what had happened. It didn't take long for him to realize how wrong he was. Though she seemed devoid of spark and untouched by the recent events, she was about to recount her story—or at least a twisted version of it. When Lockhart read her, her Miranda rights, she waived them without hesitation, agreeing to speak like it was the most natural thing in the world.

He began asking questions, but quickly noticed Angelee would only stare forward, her eyes vacant. The switch from eager compliance to this eerie blankness was the first warning of how strange the day was about to become. Trooper Blake, standing by the head of Angelee's bed, gently placed her hand on Angelee's shoulder, encouraging her to respond. Angelee turned to Blake, looked her straight in the eyes, and said, "Okay." But as Lockhart repeated the question, Angelee continued to lock eyes with Blake. When Blake repeated the question, Angelee answered without hesitation.

They soon realized that Blake had established a strange rapport with Angelee. What followed was an interview conducted through Blake—Lockhart asking the questions, Blake repeating them to get answers. It only added to the disconcerting nature of the situation.

Lockhart asked Angelee what had happened that morning, and her response was both jarring and unexpected in its stark directness. "You mean the bloodbath?" Once again, without any hesitation, she admitted to killing Bill. But as she began to recount the events, her story quickly unwound into chaos. Disjointed thoughts, fractured memories—it was impossible to follow. The detective described it as a labyrinth of twisted impressions, a path of shattered recollections that no one could walk.

Her reasoning for what had occurred was something Lockhart had never encountered in all his years on the force. Angelee claimed that electricity had guided her, that she had been driven by static, some external force beyond her control. Her words sounded more like the delusions of someone adrift in madness, but she never wavered. She spoke of these fantastical ideas with the same detachment she applied to everything else.

Lockhart explained how extracting a clear timeline from her was futile. Trying to piece together what happened was like attempting to reconstruct a shattered mirror. Angelee described hitting Bill with a lamp—perhaps more than one—as though the lamps themselves had compelled her to use them as weapons. While her words were muddled, the violence she recounted was disturbingly clear.

At some point, Angelee had held a firearm. She told Lockhart that the gun had gone off, either accidentally or prematurely. When the gun was no longer an option, she used the lamp to continue her attack. With an unnerving monotone, she described how she retrieved another firearm with the intent to shoot Bill again, but she couldn't figure out how to load or fire it. So, she beat him with it instead, striking him over and over.

The calm precision with which she recounted retrieving a large kitchen knife made everyone's skin crawl. With chilling clarity, she described stabbing Bill in the heart, believing that this had finally ended his life. She thought that at some point, she had taken the knife upstairs. She remembered Bill's desperate plea, "What are you trying to do? Kill me?" as he lay at the foot of the stairs. Even as she recounted this moment, her face remained devoid of emotion, her tone flat.

Lockhart painted a vivid picture of how the confrontation unfolded. Angelee had attempted to shoot Bill upstairs but either missed or the gun misfired. She then either pushed or kicked him, causing him to tumble down the stairs. After the fall, she knew he was still alive. It was at the bottom of the stairs that her assault continued, using whatever she could find—the lamps, the second gun, and eventually the knife.

What disturbed Lockhart the most was her acknowledgment that Bill was still alive after the fall. There was a resolute, methodical determination in the way she spoke of "finishing him off," as if it were a grim obligation. She also recounted killing Bill's dogs during the spree of violence, but like much of her story, the details were incomplete echoes of the carnage she had caused. Even among the horror of her story, there was something else that chilled Lockhart to the core. Angelee admitted that the events stretched over a long period; so long, in fact, that she had taken at least one nap during the attacks. She would lie down and rest, recuperating before resuming her assault. She wasn't sure if the nap occurred after killing Bill and the dogs or between the multiple assaults. Lockhart's voice faltered slightly as he relayed this detail to the court. The weight of her casual admission hung heavy in the air. Her mind had become so disconnected from reality that her acts of violence were nothing more than interruptions in her day.

At some point during the early morning hours, she had left the house. Bill and the dogs lay dead, and the house was a massacre waiting to be discovered. Angelee had climbed into her dark-green Tahoe and backed out of the driveway, leaving perfect tracks in the snow. She told Lockhart that the energy was still guiding her, forcing her to navigate towards an unknown destination. At peace with her thoughts, she believed she was being sent to a friend's house, but she ended up crashing into the older gentleman's car in his driveway.

In twenty-eight years of law enforcement, Lockhart admitted he had never encountered anyone quite like Angelee. Her demeanor, her words—everything was off. Disturbingly composed and matter-of-fact, she made no attempt to downplay her role. She accepted full responsibility, but the reasoning that guided her actions was bizarre and delusional. It wasn't just the content of her confession that unnerved Lockhart but also that there was a void in her confession where emotion should have been.

As I listened, the heavy reality of his words nauseated my stomach. This was my sister they were talking about. Yet, hearing about her through the eyes of a seasoned detective was almost too much to bear. He had looked into the eyes of someone utterly consumed by violence and madness, someone I thought I knew.

The burden of it all felt like an anchor dragging me down into depths I wasn't sure I could rise back up from. The fragments of this nightmare now clouded the image of the sister I grew up with. I found myself face-to-face with a reality that defied understanding—a reality that shattered any hope of reconciliation.

CHAPTER 29: BENEATH THE BLOOD

The interview was finally over. They had pushed Angelee as far as they could, extracting every piece of information she could offer. Angelee's narrative was fractured—a broken mirror reflecting a chaos of distorted images. It had been a grueling, unsettling process marked by Angelee's unwavering calmness and the frustrating gaps in her memory. Both troopers knew they had reached the point of diminishing returns; there would be no further clarity from additional questioning. She was too far removed from reality for them to piece together a coherent sequence of events. Now, with the search warrant in hand, they knew it was time to move on to the next phase.

As they prepared to collect biological samples, they meticulously reviewed the details of the warrant with Angelee. They had to execute this process with precision; the samples they gathered could provide crucial evidence in a case that was already sinister on so many levels. Wrapped in her hospital blanket, Angelee remained unaffected, waiving any rights to contest the search. But as they began their work, they quickly realized that what lay ahead would be just as challenging and just as haunting as the interview had been. This wasn't just a routine procedure, it was an intimate confrontation with the physical remnants of the unspeakable acts she had committed.

When they moved to inspect Angelee's hands, the sheer amount of blood beneath her nails took them aback. Her long nails were not just stained but were packed with thick and hardened blood. It was a grotesque sight, as if her very fingertips had been transformed by the violence she had inflicted. With each scrape of the forensic tool, chunks of the dried blood fell into the evidence envelope. The process of digging deep into the crevices of her nails was slow and painstaking. The air felt thick as the team worked in silence, exchanging glances that said more than words ever could. What they were witnessing wouldn't just be part of a report, it would linger in their minds as a lasting image of the horrors they were now entangled in.

Once they had gathered every trace of blood from her hands, they moved on to her hair. Angelee's long, curly hair was matted and stiff from the blood that had dried into thick, knotted clumps. The team worked carefully, snipping small pieces here and wetting sections there, trying to loosen the hair that had stuck together. As they combed through the tangled mess, something metallic glinted in the strands. They extracted it carefully and found a small shard of metal, instantly recognizable as a broken piece of the lamp she had used to beat Bill. The shard had flown off with such force during the assault that it had lodged in her hair like a chilling keepsake of the cruelty she had inflicted.

But the horror didn't stop there. As they continued working through her hair, another discovery sent shivers down their spines. Someone audibly said, "What is that? Is that… It is." A chunk of flesh tangled deep in her matted curls. They pulled it free, and it was undeniably flesh. The silence in the room became deafening as the team processed what they had found. When they asked Angelee about it, she looked over with a relaxed mien and said in that same flat, detached tone, "Oh, that's from the dogs."

With her hair finally free of evidence, it was time to wash away the blood that had clung to her skin. As the warm sponge moved over her body, layers of dried blood rinsed away, revealing something even more haunting beneath. At first glance, it had seemed like Angelee was tan beneath the blood, but as the sponge wiped away the layers, they realized it wasn't a tan at all. Her skin was pale, but the misting of blood was so fine and evenly distributed across her body that it had given the illusion of a tan. Trooper Blake described it as looking like an evenly applied coat of makeup foundation. The blood had seeped into every crevice, becoming a part of her, just as the violence had become intertwined with her very being.

After they had cleaned her up and gathered all the evidence, it was time to escort her to the jail for processing. Angelee remained completely unchanged as they led her to the jail. There was no resistance, no emotion, no acknowledgment of the gravity of what had happened. She complied with every instruction, moving through the intake process as if in a trance. When it came time to take her mugshot, they lined her up for the photo, and what happened next shocked everyone in the room—Angelee smiled. It wasn't a faint smile, but a cutesy, almost playful grin, as if nothing that had transpired had any bearing on her. It was a smile that froze time, a smile that encapsulated the surreal nature of everything they had witnessed. That single image was more than just a mugshot. It was a glimpse into the twisted depths of a mind that had crossed the line between reality and delusion, between innocence and unimaginable guilt.

This case wasn't just another file to be closed. What they had encountered in that hospital room and during the evidence collection was something far darker and far more troubling than any routine investigation. They had come face-to-face with someone whose actions defied reason, whose detachment from reality was as terrifying as the violence she had inflicted. The true nature of what had happened in that house would linger with them long after the case was over—a haunting reminder of the depths of human madness.

PART IV
SCENE OF THE CRIME

CHAPTER 30: THE FROZEN TRUTH

While Angelee was still at the scene of the accident before being transported to the hospital, Troopers Diez and Martin had been dispatched to the address she provided to verify if her confession held any truth. As they drove down the long, snow-covered driveway, the crunching beneath their tires was unsettling. It was the kind of snow that had melted and refrozen several times, creating a hard, brittle surface. It was eerily quiet otherwise, the winter air thick and heavy, as if the landscape itself was holding its breath. The driveway opened into a large clearing that revealed a picturesque chalet-style home. The house stood pristine, but there was something unnatural about its stillness. They parked their patrol car in front of the open garage, the door yawning wide. Inside, a large blanket lay haphazardly in the middle of the garage floor, as if tossed aside in haste or panic. The rest of the space was meticulously kept with not a tool out of place, but something was undeniably wrong.

Diez and Martin exchanged a glance as they stepped out of the car, the tension between them unspoken but tangible. The air was crisp, biting at their faces as they stood for a moment in front of the open garage, silently taking in the scene. Their eyes were drawn to the door leading from the garage into the house, where smeared streaks of blood were visible on the handle and the adjacent walls. The sight of the blood was the first undeniable sign that something terrible had occurred within. Neither of them wanted to disturb the evidence smeared on that door, and they knew whatever was on the other side needed to be approached carefully. They needed to find another way inside. Without a word, Diez gestured to Martin, silently directing him to go around to the front of the house while Diez circled around back.

Diez followed the side of the garage as it wrapped around the rear of the house, his boots crunching softly in the snow. The house backed up to a dense forest of trees, their branches sagging under the weight of snow and creating an oppressive wall of silence. His eyes scanned the exterior, taking in every detail. As he reached the back, something caught his attention: a small hole in one of the upper windows, about ten feet off the ground. The jagged edges of broken glass suggested that a bullet had punched through it. Diez's stomach sank as he called out to Martin, pointing out the discovery. Martin, still making his way from around the front, informed him that the other doors were locked. The welfare check was now unraveling into something far darker. A shot had been fired. The dread settling over them deepened.

With no other options, they returned to the garage and reluctantly decided they had no choice but to go through the blood-smeared door. The air seemed to grow heavier around them as they stood before it, both knowing that whatever lay beyond was not going to be easy to witness. Steadying themselves, they pushed the door open with a gentle touch, careful not to disturb the blood on the handle. It swung open with ease, revealing a scene that hit them like a gut punch.

Inside, the walls were streaked with more blood than they could have imagined. It wasn't just spots or smears, but full splashes and streaks that told a story of brutality. The hallway floor was covered in more blood that had dried and cracked like an old painting. A pair of scissors lay discarded in the middle of the floor, their blades coated in a dark, crusted layer of blood. The metallic scent of blood mixed with the unmistakable odor of death filled the air, turning their stomachs. It had been many hours, maybe longer, since the crime had occurred.

The sheer horror of the place seemed to pin them in place. Somehow, they pushed forward, moving cautiously through the hallway and stepping carefully around the evidence that lay at their feet. Every step was deliberate, every movement slow as they worked to preserve the crime scene while bracing themselves for what they might find.

Diez scanned the area, his senses heightened, every creak of the floorboards and drip of melting snow from the roof making his heart pound.

Martin cleared the first room off the hallway—it was empty. Diez moved towards a second room, peering through the door, and there, wedged between the bed and the wall, lay a large dog. Its body was crumpled and motionless. The animal's side bore several deep stab wounds, and the dried blood created dark patches on its coat. It was a grisly sight, the dog a silent victim of the massacre that had unfolded here.

With a growing sense of dread, they continued down the hall, which opened into a large living room, the heart of the home. The once-cozy space was now a scene of chaos.

Furniture was overturned, cushions were strewn about, and a black handgun sat ominously on the kitchen counter. A wallet lay in the middle of the floor, as if placed there on display deliberately, its contents partially spilled out. This was no ordinary crime scene; this was an eruption of violence that had torn apart a once orderly home. The chaos was fresh; it hadn't been this way for long.

Then Martin's voice cut through the silence. "I've found a body." Diez moved quickly to his side. There, sprawled on the floor, was a man, his body contorted unnaturally. Blood stained his clothes, and the unmistakable stiffness of rigor mortis had set in. Diez knelt down to check for a pulse, though he already knew it was too late. The man's skin was cold, the damage to his body horrific. The brutality was evident in every wound. Whoever this man was, he had suffered a terrible fate.

But they couldn't analyze the body any longer; they had to keep moving. There might be more victims, or worse, the perpetrator could still be inside.

With their weapons drawn, they made their way up the creaky stairs. The top of the stairs opened into a large loft, apparently the master bedroom. It was neat, orderly, almost untouched compared to the devastation downstairs. But there, next to the bed, was another large dog, its body still and lifeless. This one, too, bore signs of gore. Stab wounds punctured its side. Diez pointed silently to the bed, where a large butcher knife lay stained with blood.

With the house now fully cleared, Diez and Martin retraced their steps, exiting back through the garage. Their mission had shifted from saving lives to securing a crime scene.

As they stepped back outside into the biting cold, the morning light was beginning to brighten the horizon, casting long shadows across the snow. But the day's brightness did nothing to alleviate the weight of what they had just witnessed. They stood in the driveway, the cold air biting at their faces, their breath visible in the frigid air. And then, cutting through the silence, came the sound of tires crunching slowly over the icy snow—the distinct sound of approaching vehicles.

CHAPTER 31: SHADOWS IN THE SNOW

Trooper Stone drove up the long, worn path that stretched ahead of her. The driveway wasn't paved, just two crushed-stone tracks carved into the earth from years of vehicles passing over it. The crunch of tires against the frost-covered stones echoed in the quiet of the morning, the sound sharp in the crisp air. As she neared the house, the rustic chalet loomed into view, its serene facade starkly at odds with the horror waiting inside. Stone pulled up beside Diez's patrol car, the sight of the two officers standing in the driveway confirming what her gut had already told her—something terrible had happened here.

She stepped out of her car, the cold air biting at her exposed skin as she zipped up her coat. "So, it's true?" she asked, though the answer was clear in their grim expressions.

Diez and Martin exchanged a glance, then nodded, their faces set with the weight of what they had seen. They walked her through the details they had uncovered so far, each revelation more unsettling than the last. Stone had heard the radio call about the crime lab and coroner being dispatched, but hearing Diez and Martin recount the mayhem they had witnessed firsthand made it all feel more real and horrifying.

She couldn't connect the calm demeanor of the woman she'd spoken to at the scene of the accident with the carnage described to her now. It seemed impossible that the same person could be responsible for such an act.

Within minutes, more vehicles began to arrive. Patrol cars, their lights reflecting off the snowy ground, were followed by the crime lab van. Officers and technicians moved with purpose, their breath visible in the cold air as they started to set up near the garage. The once quiet property was now buzzing with activity, each inch of it soon to be transformed into a critical piece of evidence. The scale of the task was daunting. There were fragments of a dark story scattered everywhere, and it was up to them to gather each one and make sense of the senseless.

The investigative team worked quietly to an efficient rhythm, gathering their gear, cameras, evidence bags, and notebooks. Years of experience had taught each of them the importance of thoroughness; every detail, no matter how small, could be critical. As they moved towards the house, there was an unspoken understanding of the gravity of what they were about to witness.

The snap of a detective's latex gloves cutting through the air was a sharp reminder of the seriousness of their task. Others adjusted their gear in silence, the clink of metal on plastic the only sound to be heard. Despite having been through this routine countless times, something about this case felt different. There was a somberness to their movements, an understanding that the usual horrors of their jobs had taken on a new, darker dimension.

The lead detective gathered his team near the garage, his voice steady yet grave as he laid out the plan. The crime lab technicians would enter first and meticulously gather evidence. The rest would wait outside, mentally preparing for their own part in piecing together the timeline of events.

Stone's eyes drifted towards the garage, where a large blanket lay carelessly discarded on the concrete floor. It was out of place, a detail that seemed to mock the normalcy of a secluded home. Her mind wandered to how it had gotten there. *Had Angelee dropped it as she walked to her car, blood still covering her body?* The thought turned her stomach.

Inside, the digital cameras began their work. The constant clicking was a rhythmic reminder of just how much there was to document. Blood streaked the walls and floor near the entryway. *Click*—a photograph of the scissors discarded in the hallway, possibly an impromptu weapon. *Click*—a black pistol, carelessly left on the kitchen counter. *Click*—a wallet lying open in the middle of the floor, seemingly waiting to identify the victim it once belonged to.

The house was a tumultuous mess, as though rage itself had torn through it. Shattered lamps, overturned furniture, broken chairs and end tables littered the space. In the bedroom, the first dog was found exactly where Diez had said it would be—its fur matted with dried blood, its body eerily out of place in a room that otherwise appeared neat and untouched. It was a silent casualty of the madness that had unfolded.

Each room seemed to tell a different chapter in a dark, violent story. The team moved with precision, knowing that every inch of the house held potential clues. They couldn't afford to overlook anything. The camera's clicking persisted, capturing every angle, every disturbing detail, every fragment that might help reconstruct the unspeakable events. A technician dusted for fingerprints on doorknobs, light switches, and weapons.

Beyond gathering physical evidence, there was another pressing question. Had drugs played a role in this tragedy? The K-9 unit arrived, its handler guiding the trained dog through the house with methodical care. The dog sniffed along baseboards, furniture, and hidden crevices in search of even the faintest trace of narcotics. But there was nothing. No hidden stashes, no residue. With no drugs found, the mystery only deepened. If this wasn't a case fueled by narcotics, then what could have driven such merciless acts?

The crime lab wrapped up their part of the investigation, and the detectives moved in to begin theirs. As they prepared to dig deeper into the house's grim secrets, the coroner arrived. The time had come to respectfully transport Bill's body. Stone watched in silence as they carefully placed the lifeless form into a body bag. Even in death, the coroner handled him with dignity. The plan was to take Bill to the hospital for x-rays before moving him to the morgue, ensuring no detail was missed.

The answers they sought were still elusive, and the interview with Angelee at the hospital would be crucial. Detective Lockhart was at the hospital interviewing her, and he would need every shred of information to make sense of the senseless. They all knew that the events of this morning had shattered the peace of this quiet home, and they could only hope Angelee's account would provide some clarity.

As they left the scene, the midday sun cast short shadows over the snow-covered ground. The house stood still now, its secrets unearthed, its horrors exposed. But the cold air seemed to whisper that the hardest work was yet to come. Understanding what had happened here would require more than evidence. It would require patience, persistence, and perhaps a realization that some things could never be fully explained.

Meanwhile, a separate team was tasked with searching Angelee's vehicle, which had been towed to the impound lot. As they sifted through the contents, they found a red cord, likely the manual pull rope from the garage door. A lamp was also recovered, suspected to have been used in the crime. Then there was a furniture leg that was spattered with blood, and oddly enough, a brand-new sleeping bag that had never been used. Among the strange collection was a business card from a psychologist's office with an appointment reminder for January 19, 2021. Each of these items was logged, any one of them potentially holding the key to understanding the horror that had unfolded.

CHAPTER 32:
A HEAVY SILENCE

The judge adjourned the hearing for the evening, but the faces and voices from the courtroom stayed with me, haunting me as I walked out. Bill's family, the detectives, those poor people who had been pulled into this nightmare against their will. Each one of them carried their own version of the story, their own scars. Their faces were etched with pain, disbelief, and a gnawing hunger for answers that no one could give.

And then there was Angelee. Sitting there all distant and disconnected, her eyes glazed over as though none of this was about her. She seemed so removed, so far away from the horrific reality of what she had done. I desperately kept trying to reconcile this version of her with the little sister I had known all my life. But the woman they described in that courtroom was a stranger to me.

As we left the courthouse, the weight of the trial dragged me down like an anchor. Every revelation, every word that had been spoken felt like a punch to the gut, leaving me breathless. My mind was a storm of thoughts, swirling with shock, confusion, and a deep, aching sadness. How could it have come to this? How had Angelee, my little sister, fallen so far so fast? The same person who had been by my side through life's darkest moments was now at the heart of this terrible nightmare. The questions circled endlessly, gnawing at me, but no answers came.

Outside, the crisp air carried the familiar scent of Lake Michigan, a smell that had always brought me peace. That night, even the lake seemed cold and indifferent. The mist that kissed my skin was sharp and biting, like a harsh reminder of reality. The vast, serene lake felt distant, and its calmness seemed to mock the chaos churning inside me. My son walked beside me, our footsteps in sync and weighed down by the silence between us. I wanted to say something to him, to offer words of comfort or guidance, but I was empty. How could I possibly explain something I didn't understand myself? What could I tell him when I had no answers?

As we climbed into the car, a deep exhaustion washed over me; not just the kind that comes from a long day, but the kind that seeps into your bones. It was a weariness born from carrying too much for too long. Every muscle in my body ached, not from physical strain but from the emotional weight I had been dragging around all day. My soul felt heavy and depleted. The emotional fatigue was an invisible burden that grew with each passing hour. And I knew this was just the beginning. Tomorrow, there would be more. More testimony, more horrifying details, more pieces of the puzzle that I wasn't sure I could face. Tomorrow, the trial would dig deeper into this unthinkable nightmare, and I would have to sit through it all again.

But right then, I could only focus on the present moment. One breath, then another. The world around me continued as if nothing had changed. People were going about their evening routines, cars were passing by, the wind from the lake was rustling through the trees. For me, time had slowed to a crawl. There were no answers waiting for me tonight, no relief from the relentless sorrow. Just the dull, heavy ache of the day's events pressing down on me like a suffocating blanket. And tomorrow, I knew, it would start all over again.

CHAPTER 33: BETWEEN GRIEF AND COMPASSION

The next morning, I woke with a knot so tight in my stomach, it made me feel queasy. Sleep had come in restless fits. My exhaustion wasn't just physical, it was emotional and spiritual as well. A deep weariness seemed to cling to me. Groggy, I rolled over and reached for my phone, my hand moving almost on autopilot. The screen lit up with a message from my wife. She was checking in on me and asking me to call her when I got up.

Before I could fully digest her message, another notification caught my attention—this one from my cousin. Her words were blunt: "My mom died. Please call me."

The news hit me like a slap in the face, but with a chair. A fresh wave of shock crashed over me, piling onto the already overwhelming weight I'd carried. I sat there in bed, frozen, my mind reeling. What am I going to do? I stared at the screen, my fingers hovering over the keys, unable to find any words to respond. As I sat there, processing the blow, my son emerged from the bathroom, completely unaware of the new storm that had just rolled in.

When I told him what had happened, he stood still, shaking his head in disbelief. We both knew the hearing was expected to wrap up later that day, so we quickly adjusted our plans. As long as nothing kept us afterward, we'd head straight to southern Michigan. It didn't matter if we couldn't do anything practical—we needed to be there for my cousin.

Despite the fact that I was an emotional wreck and utterly spent, I knew we had to go. That's what family does.

I closed my eyes and took a deep, slow breath, inhaling through my nose, then exhaling just as slowly. The air felt nauseating, like even breathing was an effort. I stepped outside the room and walked out into the brisk morning air to call my wife. The coolness of the breeze stung my skin. I told her about the latest development, and though her voice was steady, I could hear the sympathy beneath her words. She offered her condolences again, understanding that the weight of this week was only getting heavier. I was barely holding it together as I explained that our trip would be extended by a few more days. *This week,* I thought bitterly, *has no intention of ending.*

When our call ended, I lingered outside for a moment, feeling the cold morning seep into my bones. I wasn't sure I could go back inside and face the day, but I had to. Back in the room, I asked my son to start packing. "Let's leave straight from the courthouse," I told him, trying to sound collected. I'd go handle the early checkout.

My mind was a chaotic swirl of thoughts, each one vying for attention, pulling me in a different direction. Angelee. The hearing. My aunt. The looming grief that awaited us at my cousin's house. It was a fog of confusion, and it made concentrating difficult as I walked through the hotel hallway. The familiar sounds of breakfast—the clinking of dishes, the hum of conversation—reached my ears, but they felt distant, like I was walking through a dream.

I entered the lobby with my head down, trying to navigate the mess of thoughts swirling in my mind, when I nearly collided with someone. "Oh, excuse me," I muttered, glancing up.

The moment our eyes met, I knew exactly who she was. I had seen her in the courtroom the day before, and from her expression, she recognized me too. My heart sank and time seemed to stretch out between us, filled with unspoken grief and shared pain.

I don't know what went through her mind in that moment, but a thousand thoughts raced through mine. All day yesterday, I had wanted to say something to Bill's family but had been too overwhelmed by the enormity of it all. Now, standing face-to-face with Bill's ex-wife, I knew the time had come to speak. My throat tightened as I forced the words out. "I'm Joe," I said, my voice trembling. "Angelee is my sister. I'm so, so sorry for your loss. I spent all day yesterday trying to find the words, but I just couldn't. I'm sorry."

Her expression softened as she introduced herself as Bill's ex-wife, then she said the last thing I expected. She mentioned her son was nearby and asked if I wanted to meet him. My stomach lurched. I knew I had to face him, but the thought of it was terrifying. I felt like I was intruding on their grief, which served as a painful reminder of everything Angelee had taken from them. I managed to say, "Yes, please."

She called her son over, and I braced myself, expecting anger or resentment. After all, Angelee had taken his father from him in the worst possible way. But when he came over, he extended his hand. I was startled by the gesture. We shook hands, and as we did, goosebumps spread across my arms. My voice cracked as I told him I had only met his father a few times, but found him to be a kind and respectful man. And then I said the only thing I could, "I'm so sorry for what my sister did."

Tears welled in both our eyes. Without thinking, I pulled him into a hug, and to my surprise, he embraced me back. In that brief moment, I felt everything—his pain, his grief, his confusion, and most shockingly, his compassion. The weight of our shared sorrow seemed to bind us, if only for that instant, as we searched for solace in the middle of this storm.

The hug lasted only a few seconds, but its impact was immense. It was a moment I knew I would carry with me forever.

As we pulled away, both of us wiped our eyes. His mother stood nearby, offering her quiet support. They spoke softly, reassuring me that they didn't blame me and that they hoped Angelee could get the help she needed. Their kindness floored me. In the face of unimaginable pain, they had found it within themselves to extend compassion. I was overwhelmed with gratitude for their grace—something I wasn't sure I deserved but needed more than I realized. My heart ached even more for them.

After our exchange, I turned and walked back to my room. My emotions were raw, my nerves exposed. I shut the door behind me and walked over to the window, where I stared out at the open field behind the hotel. The power of their unexpected compassion was replaying in my mind. My son stood nearby, watching me, waiting for some explanation as to what I was thinking. I told him what had just happened in the lobby, and he stood there, stunned by the magnitude of their grace.

After a moment, I pulled out my phone and used the app to complete our early checkout. I wasn't sure I could handle another emotional encounter. We finished packing in silence, both of us lost in our own thoughts, and slipped out through the side entrance.

As we drove away, I kept replaying the moment in the lobby—the hug, the tears, the kindness they showed. *Thank you,* I thought. *Thank you for your grace, for your mercy, for showing me what kindness looks like in the face of unimaginable grief.* I knew I would carry their example with me for the rest of my life. This small moment had changed me in ways I couldn't yet fully understand.

CHAPTER 34:
THE FINAL EXAMINATION

The atmosphere in the courtroom that morning was tense, as though the very walls were bracing themselves for the revelations to come. The previous day had taken its toll on everyone present, and everyone showed their weariness. Movements were slower, conversations quieter, and glances between people had become fewer. The heft of the testimonies from the day before still lingered, as did the heavy anticipation of what lay ahead. Today, the medical examiner was set to take the stand, and we all understood that this testimony would be the hardest to hear.

The medical examiner, a highly respected professional with over four thousand autopsies to her name, was known for her unwavering commitment to the truth and her meticulous attention to detail. She was not one to indulge in sensationalism, instead maintaining a clinical respect for the process and the people involved. Even so, nothing could prepare us for the reality of what she would reveal.

She began by outlining the procedures that took place after Bill's body was discovered. She explained how she met with the coroner at the scene, ensuring that his body was handled with the utmost respect and that the evidence was preserved. The body was transported to the hospital for x-rays. This was a necessary precaution to ensure no detail was overlooked. The imaging confirmed that there were no projectiles or bullet fragments present, which led her to conclude that he had not been shot. But this was just the start of what she was about to uncover.

The autopsy itself was scheduled for ten a.m., and an officer was present to witness the procedure. From her description, it was clear that this was no ordinary examination; it was a methodical, painstaking process that sought to unravel the violent end of a life. She described how every piece of evidence, down to the smallest fiber, was collected and documented before the actual procedure could begin. Each piece told its own story, a crucial clue in understanding what had happened.

Once the evidence collection was complete, the autopsy commenced. She detailed how she meticulously measured each wound and recorded the sharp force trauma, blunt force trauma, lacerations, and contusions. Each injury was a piece of the puzzle, telling its part of the story that led to his death. The protocol required that she work methodically, starting with the head and working her way down the body, documenting every injury with precision and care.

As she explained her findings, she made it clear that the order in which the injuries were described was not necessarily the order in which they were inflicted. Some wounds showed signs of being sustained while Bill was still alive, while others appeared to have been inflicted postmortem. The exact sequence of events remained uncertain, as there were simply too many injuries to determine such with absolute certainty. Her testimony was bound by the protocols of the autopsy, detailing the injuries from head to toe in the order dictated by the process.

As the medical examiner recounted her findings, the room seemed to close in around us. The violence was far more severe than we had imagined, and the injuries were overwhelming in their brutality. Each wound was a grim testament to the pain and struggle that had occurred. Her voice remained steady throughout. There was a clear undercurrent of respect in her tone, a quiet acknowledgment of the life that had been lost and the suffering endured.

The details were graphic and the process was painstaking, but every word carried immense heaviness. This was the final testimony for Bill, the last opportunity for someone to speak on his behalf. The medical examiner's words weren't just an account of physical evidence, they were a narrative of the unimaginable agony of Bill's final moments.

CHAPTER 35: LAYERS OF PAIN

The courtroom remained still as the medical examiner continued her testimony. She was a seasoned professional, well-versed in uncovering truths through her meticulous procedures. Yet, despite her extensive experience, it was clear that this case weighed heavily on her. The atmosphere was somber, thick with the gravity of the violence she was about to describe.

She began her account by focusing on the scalp, where she found nine lacerations and seven abrasions. She explained that some of the lacerations had distinct angular shapes, suggesting they were caused by a blunt object with a defined pattern. One of these had an L-shape, which immediately brought my mind back to Angelee's statement about using a lamp. Could that have been the source of these wounds? Then I recalled the broken piece of a lamp that was found tangled in her hair. Were these details connected?

The medical examiner clarified that these lacerations resulted from forceful blows, not from sharp instruments. She further explained the presence of "tissue bridges," which are small, unbroken blood vessels within the wound. This confirmed that the injuries were caused by blunt force rather than a clean cut.

As she moved from the scalp to the face, she described more injuries: eight lacerations and six abrasions. Some of the wounds bore specific geometric patterns that might help identify the object used to inflict them. She then discussed the fractures visible in the x-rays, particularly in the right orbital roof and at the base of the skull, which indicated a powerful impact, possibly from a strike or a fall. The nasal bone was also fractured and the cartilage dislocated. She pointed out that none of these injuries showed signs of healing, which was consistent with trauma sustained close to the time of death. While all of his teeth were intact, one had a small chip, though she couldn't conclusively say whether it had been chipped that night.

Moving on to the examination of his neck, the medical examiner revealed two shallow cutting wounds on the front of his throat, one of which had reached the thyroid cartilage, also known as the Adam's apple. However, there was no significant damage to the major blood vessels in the neck, indicating that these wounds, while serious, were not fatal. They were part of a larger, more brutal assault.

Next, she described the injuries on his right shoulder, the back of his neck, and his back. Small abrasions were present, but what caught her attention was the pattern imprinted on his skin that matched the fabric of his shirt. This suggested he had likely been lying in the same position for an extended period or had been dragged—a disturbing detail that added another layer to the already grim narrative.

Finally, she turned to the injuries on his forearms and hands. They included cuts on his fingers and bruises on the backs of his hands and forearms. These wounds, often referred to as defensive wounds, indicated that he had been trying to protect himself during the attack.

She paused for a moment, taking a sip of water. It was only then that I realized I hadn't moved since she began. My back ached, my throat was dry, and my heart raced. The room was heavy with an oppressive sense of gloom, shared by everyone present. As she set her water back down and resumed speaking, her tone unwavering, she shifted her focus to the sharp force wounds found in the upper-left area of his chest.

CHAPTER 36: THE ANATOMY OF VIOLENCE

The medical examiner spent significant time detailing the extensive injuries to Bill's upper chest and abdomen. Her findings were both thorough and deeply unsettling, painting a harrowing picture of the assault he had gone through. She began by documenting seven slit-like defects on the surface of his skin in those areas. However, as the internal examination progressed, it became clear that the damage beneath the skin was far worse and more extensive than initially expected. Within the organs—his lungs, heart, liver, chest cavity walls, and surrounding musculature—the examiner discovered more wound tracts than there were corresponding openings in the skin.

This discrepancy revealed a grim reality. Beneath each slit-like defect on the surface, multiple wound tracts had intersected and spread within the body. For example, a single slit on the upper-left chest corresponded with five separate wound tracts found in the left lung beneath the skin. She explained that this could occur if the weapon wasn't fully withdrawn before being driven back in or if it was reinserted into the same slit after being fully withdrawn. Although conclusions could be drawn, they weren't definitive. Whether this was a deliberate action or the result of chaotic violence, the result was catastrophic. The repeated force and movement of the weapon caused severe internal damage, leading to the deflation of the lung and the severing of pulmonary vessels, which caused significant bleeding into the chest cavity. Without immediate medical intervention, such a wound would have been fatal.

The examiner also identified two other wounds in the upper-left chest area. One of these had severed the subclavian vessel, a major blood vessel, leading to extensive bleeding into the surrounding soft tissue. Another wound, located on the right side of the sternum, penetrated the heart and created a narrow defect at the base of the aorta, which resulted in substantial bleeding into the pericardial sac. A similar wound on the left side of the sternum also injured the heart and thoracic aorta, contributing to additional bleeding into the left chest cavity.

The damage extended beyond the chest. Wounds on the right side of the lower chest and upper abdomen primarily affected the liver. The liver tissue had been so severely damaged that tracing the wound tracts was impossible. The examiner used the term "pulverized" to indicate that the tissue was so thoroughly destroyed that it was no longer recognizable as liver tissue. This level of destruction could have resulted from multiple penetrations or from the movement of the weapon while it was still inside the body, further compounding the internal injuries.

In addition to the liver damage, the right kidney had sustained two injuries. A large muscle that supports the back and lower spine, the psoas muscle, showed at least two identifiable wounds. Further down the body, two additional slits were found in the lower psoas muscle, denoting even more injuries that had initially gone unnoticed. The pancreas also showed damage.

One particularly disturbing detail involved a stab wound on the left side of the abdomen, which had exposed a segment of the intestinal tract—a fact noted at the crime scene.

The medical examiner also noted minor contusions and abrasions on Bill's lower extremities, including a contusion on the right shin and abrasions on the knees. Though less severe, these injuries reenforced the theory that he was in a defensive position, protecting himself during the attack.

The depth of the stab wounds was staggering, with some penetrating seven to nine inches into the body. The examiner concluded that, of the seven openings in the skin, at least four would have quickly been fatal on their own. A total of sixteen wound tracts were documented.

She concluded her testimony by determining that the cause of death was sharp force wounds to the chest and abdomen, with blunt impact head trauma as a contributory factor. The manner of death was classified as a homicide.

The clinical precision of the medical examiner's testimony, while methodical and exact, underscored the brutality and horror of the attack. Her thorough examination stood in stark contrast to the chaos and violence that had unfolded, offering a sobering perspective of the final moments of Bill's life.

I was mortified. Fighting to hold back tears—a battle I was mostly losing—I found myself paralyzed. The weight of her words hung heavy in the room, and the full reality of what had happened was almost unbearable.

CHAPTER 37:
A MOMENT OF REFLECTION

The court had tasked the Center for Forensic Psychiatry with evaluating Angelee's criminal responsibility, to determine if she had been legally insane when she committed the crimes. The prosecutor's office had arranged for an independent evaluation as well, though the defense had not sought one of their own. This is the unsettling journey into Angelee's mind, a journey that haunted me at the time and continues to break my heart as I struggle to understand.

The two psychologists were scheduled to present their testimonies via Zoom. To ensure the technology was working properly, the judge declared a recess for lunch. The room began to empty as people quietly gathered their belongings. Angelee was helped to her feet by the bailiff and walked slowly towards the door she had passed through countless times before. But this time was different. This time, she turned and caught my eye.

"I love you, Joe," she said softly. Her voice was quiet, but it reverberated across the room and struck me straight in the heart. I was stunned, immobilized by the weight of her words. Before I could even think to respond, the bailiff reminded her that she wasn't allowed to speak and gently guided her away. The door closed behind her, but her words stayed with me, echoing in my mind long after she was gone.

My son and I left the courthouse in silence, both of us still in shock from the testimony we had just heard. The idea of eating made me feel nauseous; neither of us had an appetite for anything. There was simply too much to process, too many emotions swirling inside us. I told him I had seen a park by the lake and wanted to spend our lunchtime there. He agreed and we drove in silence, hoping that the open water and fresh lake air might somehow help us make sense of everything.

The park was expansive and lined with riprap rocks where the water met the shore. Benches dotted the shoreline and a couple piers stretched out over the lake, beckoning those in need of peace or solace. The serenity of the scene felt like a temporary reprieve from the tension that had enveloped us for some time to come. We walked towards the water without speaking. After all, what words could capture the depth of what we were feeling?

I found a bench right by the water's edge and sat down. My son gestured towards the nearby pier, lifting a finger to silently letting me know he was headed that way. I nodded, watching as he walked further and further out, the distance between us growing with each step until all I could see was his silhouette against the vast backdrop of the lake. Alone with his thoughts, just like I was with mine.

As I sat there, the world around me seemed too beautiful, too serene for the darkness that hung over us. The seagulls circled and called out from above, and the rhythmic sound of waves gently lapping against the rocks offered a calm that felt out of place. I was caught between two worlds—one full of natural beauty and peace, the other full of pain and an inescapable, harsh reality waiting for us back at the courthouse.

I noticed freighter appeared on the horizon, slowly cutting across the water. For a brief moment, I allowed myself to be lost in the scene, grateful for the temporary distraction. Then a realization hit me with crushing force: Angelee may never see this again. She may never feel the cool breeze from the lake, never watch the seagulls fly overhead, never lose herself in the beauty of the world. Her life might be confined to the sterile, suffocating walls of a prison cell, her mind locked in a reality I could never fully understand. That thought sunk heavily in me. It was almost too much to bear.

A sudden, vivid memory came to the surface. Angelee was just a little girl, maybe four or five. We had been playing in an old refrigerator box, pretending it was a fort in the middle of the living room. I jumped out, and the box tipped over with her still inside. She hit her head on the corner of our big, old, floor model TV. The panic that followed came back to me in full force. She lay there screaming, blood pouring from a cut on her head. Mom rushed her to the hospital, and I was terrified. I was supposed to protect her, and instead, I'd hurt her. She came home hours later with seven stitches in her head. I hadn't thought of that moment in decades. But now, sitting on there on that bench, the memory returned with startling clarity. Had I let her down even back then? The helplessness I felt that day was nothing compared to the overwhelming helplessness I felt now.

My son returned from the pier, his steps slow and deliberate. He sat down next to me, and we talked quietly, our voices blending with the sound of the waves. We spoke about the hearing, about Angelee, about Bill and his family. We shared memories—some happy, some painful—and reflected on how quickly life could change. The sadness between us was easy to see, but beneath it was a deep sense of gratitude for one another. We were thankful for the strength we had found in facing this unimaginable situation together.

That moment by the lake with my son was significant to me. We were still burdened with everything, but for that time, there was a sense of peace. I was thankful for his presence, his quiet strength, and the knowledge that no matter what lay ahead, we would face it together.

Before long, it was time to return to the courthouse, to face the final chapter of what had been an agonizing hearing. Those moments by the lake had given me a brief reprieve from the frenzy of information we heard, but I knew it was the calm before the storm. We stood up, took one last look at the water, and walked back to the car. Side by side, we would get through whatever was waiting for us.

CHAPTER 38: SHATTERED REALITY

A forensic psychologist from the Center for Forensic Psychiatry was the next to take the stand, via Zoom. With a wealth of experience, he had conducted over nine hundred forensic evaluations. His expertise in assessing criminal responsibility was immediately evident. His role in this case was crucial: to determine if Angelee met the legal criteria for insanity at the time the crimes were committed. It was a complex and delicate task, one that would require a thorough examination of her mental state during the offenses.

The psychologist explained that a *criminal responsibility evaluation*, also known as an insanity evaluation, is a legal assessment to determine whether a defendant was mentally ill to the point of not understanding their actions at the time of the crime. It focuses on whether the defendant had the capacity to appreciate the nature of their actions or comprehend their wrongfulness. This legal definition of insanity is stringent, and meeting it requires clear evidence that the individual's mental state was severely impaired at the time of the offense.

His process was methodical and thorough. He began by reviewing all available police reports. Those included were from the Michigan State Police, Cadillac Police, and the Manistee County Sheriff's Office. He also carefully listened to the 911 call recordings and gathered Angelee's previous mental health and medical records. After this comprehensive review, he conducted a detailed interview with Angelee from the jail. This interview was a critical component of his assessment, as it allowed him to directly observe her behavior, listen to her account of the events, and assess her mental state.

Once he completed his rigorous evaluation, the psychologist's conclusion was clear and unequivocal: Angelee met the legal definition of insanity. He stated that she was indeed legally insane at the time of the crimes. Not only that, but he emphasized that his conclusion was not a close call. Forensically speaking, it was very clear to him that her mental state had been severely compromised. He described her mental deterioration, highlighting delusions that consumed her. Angelee believed the Purge was imminent and that she was being spied on through satellites inside her home. She thought the electric grid was being manipulated to send her messages, forcing her to prove her worth to avoid being killed.

The psychologist further explained that Angelee was experiencing intense psychotic symptoms at the time of the crimes and was not on any medication. I could barely grasp what I was hearing. *Was this really about my sister?* How had she slipped so far into this without anyone realizing? He noted that one of the key pieces of evidence supporting his conclusion was the 911 call made prior to the crimes. During the call, Angelee articulated the same bizarre delusions that had driven her actions. This consistency across different sources of evidence—her statements to the police, her behavior during the crime, and the content of the 911 call—all reinforced his assessment that her actions were not based in reality but were the result of a deeply disturbed mind.

When he was questioned by the prosecutor about the possibility of malingering, which refers to the intentional faking or exaggerating of mental illness to avoid responsibility, he was firm in his response. He explained that his extensive experience had equipped him with the ability to distinguish between genuine psychotic disorders and cases where individuals might be attempting deception. He was vigilant about this possibility and always on the lookout for inconsistencies that may suggest deception.

Could she really be this far gone? I couldn't help but feel lost, struggling to comprehend how the sister I had known my entire life could become the person now being described in such stark, clinical terms. Was she even aware of the horror she had unleashed? In Angelee's case, her symptoms and behaviors were consistent with a genuine psychotic disorder, and there was no evidence to suggest that she was malingering. Dating back to 2019, her mental health records provided further support for this conclusion.

While the psychologist did not offer a specific diagnosis as part of his evaluation, he indicated that Angelee's symptoms were most consistent with schizophrenia. He stated that schizophrenia and similar psychotic disorders are complex conditions with no single cause. He explained that research suggests they result from a combination of genetic predisposition and environmental stressors. Although schizophrenia has a strong genetic component, it doesn't always manifest across generations. In some cases, substance abuse can exacerbate or trigger psychotic symptoms, but there was no evidence of substance use playing a role in Angelee's case.

He discussed the episodic nature of psychotic disorders like schizophrenia, which means that individuals can experience intense periods of psychosis—where their thoughts and behavior are disconnected from reality—followed by intervals where they may appear to function more normally, especially if they are on medication. He noted that individuals with these disorders often struggle with social engagement and may have difficulty understanding interactions or perceiving their environment accurately. They can attribute special or personalized meaning to things that aren't based in reality, further complicating their ability to function in society.

The testimony concluded with the psychologist noting that Angelee's mental state had become much more stable since she began consistently taking her prescribed antipsychotic and anxiety medications. This stability underscored the episodic nature of her condition and highlighted the critical importance of proper medical treatment in managing her symptoms.

Wait, what?! A psychotic break? A psychotic episode? Schizophrenia? What in the hell is happening? I was always under the impression she was just fighting depression and dealing with extreme mood swings. How could this be something entirely different? Could she have been slipping into this all along, right in front of us? Why did nobody see it? How could we not have seen it? My mind was spinning, trying to grasp what I was hearing. My God, I was completely blindsided by this. Even after listening to all the testimony, I had no idea this is where it was leading.

My heart felt like it was shattering into a million pieces. How could it keep breaking like this? I stared at the back of her head as the testimony ended, just staring, trying to make sense of it all. The tears kept coming, and I couldn't stop them. How could this be possible? Insanity pleas, psychosis, delusions—these were things I had only seen on TV, distant concepts that never touched my life. But now? Now they were crushing me. I didn't know what to think, what to feel.

Mental health—it's so much more real, so much darker and deeper than I ever knew. I was completely shattered inside, and I had no idea how to put the pieces back together.

CHAPTER 39:
THE FINAL WITNESS

The prosecution had sought an additional, independent evaluation of Angelee. The testimony of the independent forensic psychologist helped to further understand Angelee's mental state at the time of the crimes. The courtroom listened intently as the seasoned psychologist, who had conducted countless forensic evaluations, began his testimony.

From the outset, the psychologist was asked if he had reached a conclusion regarding her mental state. He confirmed that he had, and began explaining that Angelee did suffer from severe mental illness. His investigation had uncovered compelling evidence that her condition had significantly worsened in the time leading up to the crimes. He mentioned the particularly powerful 911 calls made prior to the incident, as well as observations of her behavior by the arresting officers and later during her time in jail. He said these were crucial in forming his opinion.

The psychologist emphasized the importance of the 911 calls, describing them as a window into Angelee's deteriorating mental state. In these calls, she was clearly distressed, seeking help, and demonstrating signs of severe mental illness. This distress, along with her erratic behavior observed by law enforcement and jail staff, indicated that she was not in touch with reality.

He also went on to explain that his evaluation led him to conclude that Angelee was suffering from a substantial disorder of thought and mood during the time in question. The psychologist's task was to determine whether this illness impaired her ability to understand the nature and quality of her actions, and whether she could appreciate the wrongfulness of her conduct.

After carefully analyzing the facts of the case, he concluded that Angelee's actions were not rooted in reality. There was no rational, reality-based motivation for the crimes she committed. Her thoughts and behavior were grossly disorganized, influenced by a psychotic state that included delusions—both paranoid delusions and delusions of reference. Delusions of reference involve a belief that benign or random events carry specific, often personal, significance. In Angelee's case, these delusions, coupled with her paranoia, drove her actions in a way that was detached from reality.

He stressed that the desperation was evident in the 911 calls Angelee made, and that they were a key factor in his analysis. The calls, along with consistent reports from others who had witnessed her behavior, strongly supported the conclusion that Angelee was suffering from severe mental health issues at the time of the crimes. When asked whether this was a "close call" in determining her legal insanity, his response was unequivocal.

"In my opinion," he stated, "this was not a close call. There is very strong support for a finding of legal insanity." He clarified that he had considered all possible alternative explanations, leaving no stone unturned in his evaluation.

After his thorough investigation, he reiterated his firm belief that Angelee was unable to appreciate the nature and quality—or the wrongfulness—of her actions. Furthermore, he asserted that she could not conform her behavior to the requirements of the law due to the severe and acute symptoms she was experiencing during that time.

The significance of his findings hung over the courtroom, casting a somber and oppressive silence. His professional opinion, supported by extensive evidence and careful consideration, painted a disturbing picture of Angelee's mental state during the events in question.

CHAPTER 40:
THE 911 CALL

There had been more than one occasion during the trial when people referred to the 911 call(s), but nothing could have prepared me for hearing it myself. Listening to that call was like being struck by lightning—a jolt of raw, uncontrollable emotion surging through me, leaving me paralyzed in my seat. I had braced myself for it, but no amount of preparation could shield me from hearing my sister's voice in such a desperate, fractured state. It wasn't just a recording; it was a haunting glimpse into the dark, turbulent world Angelee was trapped in, and the horror of it all was almost too much to bear.

The courtroom, already thick with emotion, became even more oppressive when the recording played. The air seemed to grow heavier, making it difficult to breathe. Angelee's voice echoed through the room, slightly distorted by the recording, yet unmistakably hers. The fear and confusion in her tone was gut-wrenching. She sounded terrified, as if she were lost in a nightmare she couldn't wake from. The calm, methodical voice of the 911 operator stood in stark contrast to her frantic plea. Angelee wanted them to come and take the gun from her. She said she knew what "they" were doing, that she was tired of playing "their" twisted game. There was a chilling certainty in her words, as if she truly believed someone or something was manipulating her, driving her to the edge.

Her voice wavered between panic and determination as she told the operator, "I don't want to be part of their experiment anymore. They've been controlling me, but I see it now." There was an eerie certainty in her words as she continued, "Everything is a simulation. Nothing is real, and I know better now.

Please, come get the gun out of my hand." She repeated the plea, her tone growing more frantic, "I don't want it anymore. I need out, I need to escape from this." There was a sense of finality in her voice, as if she believed this was her only way to break free from the invisible forces she thought had been influencing her all along.

I wish I could remember every word, every inflection, but the truth is, I was overwhelmed. The flood of emotions—anger, sorrow, fear, and confusion—was too much to process. My memory of the call is more of a visceral feeling than a clear recollection. It wasn't just her words; it was the panic in her voice that tore at me. This was my sister—my little sister—the same girl I had grown up with, now reduced to a frightened, broken person pleading for help in a way I had never heard before.

As the recording continued, I glanced at Angelee. She sat motionless, her eyes fixed somewhere in the distance, as though the call wasn't her own, as though she were disconnected from it all. The shackles binding her wrists and ankles were a stark reminder that this wasn't a nightmare we could wake up from. This was her life now. The armed bailiff stood behind her, a silent but undeniable presence, acknowledging the risk she still posed, even in this state.

The call was only a fragment of the original, but it was more than enough. The weight of it pressed down on me, suffocating me as I tried to comprehend how we had reached this moment. Hearing her voice filled with fear and desperation was like a blow to the gut. The sister I had known, the one I had shared a childhood with, was lost somewhere in that voice, buried beneath layers of paranoia and terror.

That recording is seared into my memory—not for the exact words spoken, but for the raw, unfiltered emotion that poured out of it. It was a moment that encapsulated the tragedy of it all—Angelee's descent into madness, the horrifying actions that followed, and the heartbreaking realization that the person I had once loved so deeply was lost, perhaps forever.

CHAPTER 41: CLOSING STATEMENT OF THE PROSECUTION

The last witness had been called and was finished. The judge now started to speak. He said that we were here over the last two days to determine whether Angelee's not guilty by reason of insanity plea to all charges should be accepted by the court. He asked the prosecutor if he had any closing statement. He did.

Here are direct quotes from the transcripts of his closing statement:

"Your Honor, the Court has sat here for the last day and a half and looked at the exhibits and listened to the testimony, and in some case actually listened to the exhibit. There isn't anything that I can say that would be more compelling than the chilling testimony in evidence that the Court has seen and heard over these last days.

"There's been ample evidence to prove that the defendant, Ms. Ross, murdered William Johnson, and that she killed the two dogs willfully and without just cause. I think that's been presented very clearly, and during that entire incident it's also clear that she possessed a firearm, based upon the testimony likely more than one given what was found at the scene.

"The statute and the case law requires the firearm be accessible and obtainable during the felony, she doesn't necessarily have to have it on her person the whole time, although I believe that during the course of this the evidence was she would have had it on her person.

"There's certainly — one of the charges, your Honor, is open murder, and there's been more than ample evidence of certainly Murder 2, but I also think that there is evidence of premeditation, specifically if the Court looks to the statements of 'she had to finish him off', "beat him until he stopped moving', I think there was a statement of 'beat him with things until he stopped moving then stabbed him among other things.'

"If the Court looks to the testimony and the evidence, it appears there were multiple attempts by the defendant to kill Mr. Johnson, she wasn't successful at first, and when you look at the scene it appears that this went on for some time, we don't know how long, but if the court looks to Mr. Johnson's home and the things — the furniture that's flipped over, many of those things appear to have been done during the struggle. Is it possible some of these things could have been done afterwards? Yes. But many of those things, including the broken lamps, there was evidence that at one point this started upstairs and ended downstairs.

"So with all of those things I certainly think that this Court could make a finding that it has been shown that she committed first degree murder. I think there's ample justification on the record for that.

"Either way, your Honor, the evidence and testimony does show that she murdered Mr. Johnson, that she killed both dogs without cause, and that she did indeed possess a firearm during the course of these felonies.

"Now, as to her mental state, the evidence speaks basically for itself. The Court has sat through much of the testimony. Obviously the doctors' testimony of the two different doctors was clear as was some of the behaviors that were exhibited by the defendant during the course — well actually, the events leading to this incident and also during the course of the investigation by law enforcement.

"So your Honor, based upon everything, I would ask this Court to make appropriate findings."

CHAPTER 42: CLOSING STATEMENT OF THE DEFENSE

"We do not dispute that the evidence has clearly shown that Ms. Ross committed the crimes that she's charged with having been — having committed. I will leave it to the Court's discretion to make a determination about the — whether it would be first degree murder or whatever — whatever.

"I agree that some of the evidence could be looked at as revealing some level of premeditation, but it would also appear that, given the severity of her mental illness at the time, that she may not have been capable of such a thing.

"The evidence, as [Mr. Prosecutor] just pointed out, was compelling. Even single officer who testified indicated that it was clear to them that Ms. Ross was suffering from a severe mental illness at the time that she was interviewed by them just shortly after the killing of Mr. Johnson. Several of the officers indicated that in their 20-plus years of service they have not seen anything more incredible than what they observed in this case.

"The Court is aware that this is a plea-taking proceeding that requires the Court to first determine that the acts were committed as charged, and second, to determine by a — to determine that the defense has shown by a preponderance of the evidence that Ms. Ross was legally insane at the time.

"We heard the doctors discuss the definition of insanity. MCL 768.21a indicates that an individual is legally insane if as a result of mental illness as defined in Section 400 of the Mental Health Code, that person lacks substantial capacity either to appreciate the nature and quality, or the wrongfulness of his or her conduct, or to conform his or her conduct to the requirements of the law.

"The definition, in turn, of mental illness, is a substantial disorder of thought or mood which significantly impairs judgement, behavior, capacity to recognize reality, or ability to cope with the ordinary demands of life.

"And again, your Honor, the evidence that has been presented in this Court has been compelling, it has shown by well over a preponderance of evidence, clear and convincing — plus evidence that Ms. Ross was indeed mentally ill and legally insane at the time of these events.

"We would ask the Court to accept her plea of not guilty by reason of insanity."

CHAPTER 43:
THE GAVEL SWINGS

This was it. The Judge was about to address the courtroom. My pulse quickened, my heart pounding in my chest. Beads of sweat formed on my brow, a physical manifestation of the emotional storm raging inside me. My heart was shattered, fragmented by the revelations of everything we had been through. My emotions were scattered, veering wildly between despair and sorrow, not just for Angelee, but for Bill's family and for my son, who had stood by my side through this unimaginable ordeal.

I hadn't even begun to process the torrent of new information we'd been bombarded with over the past two days—information so raw and graphic that it left me questioning the world I thought I knew.

The judge started speaking.

"I would just like to begin and observe that we've had a number of people in the gallery. I suspect we have family and friends and people here supporting one side or the other, and you are all in my thoughts as we conclude this hearing."

He went on to explain each of the six charges, and what it is explicitly that the court must look for and find in order to accept the plea.

"Now, returning to the first question before the Court today, is there evidence that establishes support for finding that this defendant has committed the acts charged, one doesn't have to look beyond the defendant's own words to [previous witnesses] during separate interviews conducted by each of the police officers. This defendant acknowledged killing William Johnson.

"Then when you start to examine further how that killing was committed, it appears from the evidence she first attempted to use a handgun; that was unsuccessful. There was physical violence, there was bludgeoning with an instrument that caused the injuries that [medical examiner] described finding to the head area of Mr. Johnson, and ultimately there were the multiple stab wounds to Mr. Johnson's thoracic cavity and his stomach. Although there were, as I understood [medical examiner]'s testimony, only seven openings, there were numerous wound paths within the body cavity that was discovered during the post-mortem investigation.

"So this was not a single gunshot, it wasn't a single stab, it wasn't a single bludgeoning, it was this display of rage over a period of time that ultimately appears to have led to Mr. Johnson's death, and if you apply what I've just read, the elements of first degree premeditated murder and the previous court's guidance as to how to determine whether this was a deliberate act or the act was premeditated, I'm satisfied that there is more than enough evidence before the Court considering the investigation, [medical examiner]'s testimony and, again, returning to the defendant's own statements to the officers that there is sufficient support for finding that this defendant committed the crime of first degree premeditated murder."

He also went on to discuss that there was sufficient evidence for finding that she killed the two dogs without just cause.

It was found that with the bullet hole in the window and stair landing, along with the actual bullet in the tree branch that was recovered, there was sufficient evidence that she carried or had possession of a firearm at least at some point during the felonious crime.

Then came the "Second Prong" demonstrating by a preponderance of evidence that she was legally insane at the time of the offense. This was accepted by the Court through the doctors' testimonies, the 911 calls, the laypersons' testimonies, the police officers, and the defendants own words.

The judge turned to Angelee and said, "As I explained to you, Ms. Ross, you understand that if I now accept your not-guilty-by-reason-of-insanity pleas, again, I'm required to commit you to the Center for Forensic Psychiatry for up to 60 days, and then the Center will prepare a report, and it's very possible, and I would suggest you should anticipate, that I will be ordered to direct — or it will be recommended that I direct the Prosecuting Attorney to proceed in the probate court and pursue involuntary commitment proceedings in the probate court for Manistee County with regards to you, do you understand that?"

Angelee replied, "I understand that."

The judge continued, "And that may result in your being hospitalized for the rest of your life, do you understand that as well?"

Angelee said, "I understand."

Just like that, it was over. The judge said a few more words to the attorneys, something about submitted evidence, but I couldn't focus on the details. I was frozen in my chair, unable to move, still trying to process everything that had just happened. I watched as the bailiff helped Angelee to her feet one last time. She walked out without looking up, and this time, she never looked back.

CHAPTER 44: A JOURNEY TO UNDERSTANDING

Over the past two and a half years, Angelee and I have spoken perhaps a couple dozen times. She's currently being held in a Michigan mental health facility, and I'm relieved to see her working through the acceptance of what happened and finding some peace. Therapy and medication have brought stability to her mental health, and as I processed everything that has transpired, I found the strength to visit her. During our visit, I saw the woman I once knew. When she laughed, it was the comforting reminder I needed of that little girl who could always bring a smile to my face.

Yet, as I sit here reflecting on my recent visit, there's a thought that refuses to leave me: Bill's family will never have the chance to visit with him again. That reality weighs heavily on my heart, a burden I now know Angelee carries as well.

My thoughts often drift to Bill's family, especially his son. I can't begin to understand the depth of their grief. It haunts me, knowing that no words—mine or anyone else's—will ever truly heal their pain. The sorrow I feel for them is indescribable, yet I know it pales in comparison to the anguish they must endure daily.

During our visit, I found out that Angelee does remember what happened. She knows, and she holds an immense amount of guilt trying to comprehend it. She's processing it with the help of her care team as she's learning to live with her illness.

For me, everything I learned about mental health during the trial was eye-opening, but what I've learned since has been life-altering.

Schizophrenia is far more common than I had ever realized, and understanding it fully will take me much longer.

Before this, I never understood how someone could live in a reality that doesn't exist. I thought the line between real and unreal was always obvious, but now I know it can blur so easily for those suffering from illnesses like schizophrenia. The voices, the visions—everything feels so real to them. This realization shook me to my core, forcing me to confront how little I truly understood about the struggles people face within their own minds.

I've since watched, read, and listened to countless stories from those who suffer from this illness, and their experiences align exactly with what I witnessed in that courtroom. Grasping the sheer prevalence of schizophrenia in the world today has left me saddened. There must be so many people out there like me who simply don't understand and don't know how to help. During our visit, I asked Angelee the question that had been burning inside me: how could someone have helped her before the unthinkable happened? Her response was shockingly simple. "Take me. Force me to go to the hospital," she said, staring directly into my eyes, her answer firm and without hesitation.

I pushed back, just a little. "Wouldn't you have been pissed? How can someone be sure it's time to go to the hospital? It's terrifying to take someone against their will, especially when you're not certain something is wrong." Her response came wrapped in newfound clarity, delivered with the kind of confidence that only comes after a long journey of self-reflection. "If you think it's time, it is."

Her words hit me hard. I leaned back, running my fingers across my chin, trying to absorb what she had just said. Could it really have been that simple? Could forcing her to get help have prevented all of this? The thought was terrifying—knowing that action might have made a difference, but only realizing it in hindsight. My stomach twisted with guilt and fear. "That's scary, Angelee," I finally whispered.

She held my gaze, her eyes heavy with sorrow. "Joe, it's not as scary as what happened."

She was right, of course. Even though we hadn't spoken much before the tragedy, I found myself wishing I had been there to notice the signs. So many people suffer in silence, hidden in the shadows, their struggles invisible to the outside world.

As I mentioned earlier, Angelee remembers that night, and the agonizing time leading up to it. In the interest of understanding, it's crucial to understand what she saw and heard, and how her mind gradually unraveled, taking control in ways none of us could have imagined. In sharing her story here, I hope to offer a window into the torment of being trapped within your own mind—where reality blurs and you become a prisoner of your own thoughts, lost and unable to find a way out.

The words that follow, are straight from Angelee herself; as she says she remembers.

PART V

CHAPTER 45: LOST IN YOUR OWN PARANOIA

Angelee told me about when things first started to feel off for her. She was managing a small discount store, and for a while, she was actually happy there. She liked the routine, enjoyed the work, and had a nice sense of purpose. But then, things started to shift, and she said, looking back, that's where the first real symptoms began. There was this constant uneasy feeling she just couldn't shake. It wasn't the kind of stress that comes and goes; it settled in deep, and it kept growing.

At first, it was just small things. She'd be set on edge by some small reason, like the sound of a door creaking open, or the way a customer would glance at her for a moment too long. But after a while, the feelings grew stronger, sharper. She told me she started to feel like people were watching her, even when she was alone. She said she noticed her employees acting strangely— exchanging glances and whispering when they thought she wasn't around. At some point, one specific thought started to take hold: What if they were trying to hurt her?

The breaking point came over something as simple as a drink. She always kept a water bottle nearby, like most of us do, just to sip on during the day. One afternoon, she set it down on the desk in her office and walked away to help a customer. When she came back, she noticed the cap wasn't screwed on tightly. She said she hesitated for a moment feeling a strange twinge of anxiety, but she tried to brush it off. She picked up the bottle, loosened the cap, and took a drink.

It didn't take long before she started feeling sick, really sick. Her stomach twisted with painful cramps, and a wave of nausea came over her that made her sit down. She said she felt like her entire body was rebelling against her. That was when she became convinced that someone had poisoned her. It wasn't just a passing thought; it took root in her mind like a fact.

She left the store, her hands trembling on the steering wheel as she drove home to her apartment. It wasn't long before she knew she had to call 911. An ambulance came and took her to the emergency room. She told me every bump in the road seemed to make the pain worse. She said her thoughts raced in time, synced with the beating of her heart. It pounded out the certainty that she'd been poisoned, that someone was trying to kill her. By the time she reached the hospital, she was convinced she was in real danger.

At the emergency room, she told them everything: how she was feeling, what she thought had happened, and even her suspicions about her employees tampering with her drink. She said the doctors and nurses took her seriously at first. The police got involved as well; they even took her drink as evidence and sent it off for testing. For a moment, she said, she felt a strange sense of relief, as the fact that they were investigating meant that her fears were validated.

But the tests came back clean. There was nothing in the drink—no poison, no drugs, nothing that could explain what she was feeling. The doctors told her she was fine, at least physically. They tried to reassure her, but she said their calm voices only made her more afraid. It felt dismissive, like they didn't really believe her, or worse, that they were part of whatever was going on.

After that day, she said, the paranoia didn't go away. If anything, it grew stronger. She stopped trusting her coworkers and began seeing threats everywhere—in sounds, shadows, little things that didn't make sense but somehow seemed connected. She told me it was like walking through a fog where nothing was clear and everything felt dangerous.

She says that looking back now, she can see how the delusions took root and how the paranoia spread. But at the time, she was absolutely convinced. She was sure someone was out to harm her, and nothing anyone said could change her mind.

CHAPTER 46: LIVING IN A SIMULATION

In the days leading up to that tragic night, Angelee's world felt like it was closing in. She became consumed with the belief that she was trapped in a simulation, where every movement she made was tracked and every word she spoke was overheard. The thought of being under constant surveillance gripped her mind like a vice, tightening with each passing day. It wasn't just paranoia, it felt like a horrifying certainty. She was convinced that people were lurking behind the scenes, orchestrating it all, using the most ordinary objects to monitor her every move. As the fear grew, it became unbearable, pressing down on her like a weight she couldn't escape. She felt like she was suffocating, and she knew she had to take action if she was going to protect herself and Bill.

Her efforts began with a frantic urgency. She tore through both her and Bill's houses with a singular focus, ripping smoke detectors from the ceilings and walls. Each one felt like an enemy she had to neutralize. Her hands shook as she unscrewed them, the plastic casing cool and smooth beneath her fingertips. As she tore them down, she imagined tiny microphones hidden inside, capturing every whisper and every breath. Each time a detector came loose and she threw it to the floor, it felt like a small victory—a momentary release from the invisible grip of those watching her. But the relief was fleeting. The feeling of eyes on her was still there, prickling the back of her neck. It wasn't enough.

The microwaves were next. She approached them with a pounding heart, as if they were living things that might come to life and betray her secrets at any moment. She yanked the plugs from the walls with a desperate force, her breath coming in short gasps. She knew it was ridiculous to think that kitchen appliances could be used against her, but her fear didn't care about reason. In her mind, these machines were tools of the simulation, capable of picking up conversations and sending them to whoever was controlling everything. She felt a dark satisfaction each time a plug came loose, the hum of the appliance falling silent. It was one less way for them to listen.

No matter how many devices she dismantled, though, the feeling wouldn't leave her. The sense of being constantly observed lingered, like an itch beneath the skin she couldn't scratch. That's when Angelee's thoughts turned to the cameras on her computer and phone. Those tiny, unblinking lenses were like eyes, silently watching her every move. She could almost feel them on her, studying her, even when the screens were dark. She snatched up a roll of electrical tape, her hands trembling as she tore off strips and pressed them over the cameras, smoothing the tape down with shaky fingers, as if creating a shield against the watchers. It was a small comfort, but it wasn't enough to calm the dread that had taken root deep inside her.

She would look up at the night sky and see the satellites moving across the darkness. To most people, they were just distant points of light, but to Angelee, they were something far more sinister. She was certain they were part of the surveillance, broadcasting her life in real-time for others to see. She imagined them beaming down live streams of her every movement, broadcasting her private moments on social media, specifically Facebook. In her mind, it wasn't just possible—it was happening. It was all part of a grand, twisted scheme, and she was at the center of it with her life being laid bare for an audience she couldn't see.

As each day passed, Angelee's attempts to fight back against the surveillance became an all-consuming obsession. She would pace from room to room, her eyes darting to every corner, her ears straining to catch any sound out of place. Her heart raced whenever she thought she saw a glint of light reflecting off a window, convinced it was a sign that they were still watching. She was fueled by a desperation to reclaim some sense of control in a world that seemed to be slipping further into chaos, a world where every step felt like a step closer to madness.

Her actions, though frantic and erratic, were an attempt to protect herself and Bill from a threat she was certain was real. But instead of finding safety, all she uncovered was the dark, bottomless well of her own fear—a fear that consumed everything, leaving no room for reason or reassurance.

CHAPTER 47: DRIVEN BY DELUSIONS

Angelee told me that on that night that she was absolutely certain the Purge was real. The feeling was so intense, so all-consuming that it didn't feel like a delusion; it felt like reality itself had shifted. In her mind, the world outside had already descended into chaos, and they had to be ready for the violence that was sure to come.

She had been waiting for Bill to get home from work, and as the time went on, she dozed off in the backseat of her car. When he finally arrived, he woke her up, and the urgency came flooding back. She told him right away that they needed to prepare, to get everything ready for what was about to happen. She said Bill didn't question her—at least not out loud. They went into the house together, and without hesitation, he pulled out three guns and started loading them, as if he believed her completely.

Angelee said that gave her a twisted sense of relief, almost like validation. It was a confirmation that she wasn't the only one who saw the impending danger, that maybe, just maybe, she wasn't imagining things after all.

As soon as Angelee got inside, she raced to the breaker box and flipped all the switches, plunging the house into complete darkness. She told me that in her mind, cutting the power was the only way to stay safe. It would keep them hidden and make it harder for anyone to find them.

Bill didn't seem to question it; he went along with her plan. They crouched low by the windows, side by side, peering out into the dark woods. She said they whispered back and forth, going over how they'd defend themselves if someone tried to break in, mapping out different scenarios like soldiers preparing for battle.

The hours dragged on, and the tension thickened with every passing minute. Angelee said she could feel it in the air, a heavy charge that seemed to buzz in her bones. Then she saw something that sent her heart racing. The condensation in the house began to lift, rising from the floors, the furniture, even the windows. It swirled upward like steam, and in that moment, she was sure she knew what was happening. To her, there was only one explanation: someone was trying to get them by overloading the house with electricity.

"The house is overcharging!" she shouted, panic breaking through in her voice.

That was when everything shifted. Angelee said she heard a clear and urgent voice whispering, "He's turned against you. He's going to kill you!" It was like a switch had flipped inside her, and the fear she'd been feeling instantly morphed into something darker, something more intense—pure survival instinct.

She had been holding the gun while keeping watch over the house, and at that moment, she fired the first shot. It echoed through the darkened rooms, but she missed. Bill spun around, his voice booming, "You can't be shooting that in the house!"

She said there was no time to think, no chance to question what was happening; there was only energy coursing through her body in pure desperation. Without hesitation, the energy forced her at him, shoving him down the stairs. The sound of his body thudding against each step was deafening.

She rushed down the stairs after him, grabbed a lamp, and swung it hard, striking him in the head. He stumbled, then turned, and they began to struggle. But Bill was stronger. He managed to pin her down, straddle her, and delivered three solid punches to her head and face. The pain was sharp and immediate, but Angelee said there was something else, something that made the situation feel even more hopeless. In the middle of the fight, she lost control of her bladder, wetting herself. It was humiliating, like her own body had turned against her when she needed strength the most.

Then, just as suddenly as it started, Bill stopped and stepped back. She couldn't tell whether he thought he'd finally subdued her or if he was feeling some regret for what he'd done. He turned and started towards the breaker box to restore the power. But in that moment, none of that mattered. She saw her chance and took it.

She grabbed a lamp from the table and swung it with all the strength she had left, the base connecting with the side of his head. The impact made him stumble, and she bolted up the stairs, her mind racing. In that moment, there was no doubt left—Bill was one of them, and he was coming for her. She said she could feel it in her bones, that cold certainty that he was after her, and that it was either him or her.

Angelee told me she grabbed the butcher knife they had brought upstairs earlier, thinking they might need it if things got bad. She waited, her hands trembling as she listened to Bill's footsteps coming up the stairs. As soon as he reached the top, she lunged forward and shoved him back down. This time, when he hit the bottom, he didn't move.

She said she stood there for a moment, frozen, not sure if he was dead or alive. But then something in her snapped, and she ran down to him, the knife gripped tightly in her hand. She told me that when she started stabbing, it was like everything else fell away. The room, the darkness, even the weight of the knife in her hand—it all disappeared. She doesn't remember how many times she did it or the exact moment when he stopped breathing. All she remembers is the voice she heard in her head. It was calm and commanding, telling her to "finish the job."

She said that's when she knew what she had to do next. She didn't even question it. She found the dogs and killed them, just like the voice told her to. Then she grabbed a blanket, laid down and slept.

When she woke up, still wrapped in the warmth of the blanket she'd slept in, an overwhelming sense of urgency hit her. It was more than just a fleeting thought; it was a primal instinct, a deep pull in her gut that screamed she had to leave, now. Her heart raced as confusion mingled with an unshakable certainty that she had to act. There was no time to think, no time to question the sudden panic that had overtaken her. It wasn't about understanding but about following that invisible force that seemed to push her onward, demanding she move.

She stumbled through the garage, her steps quick and unsteady. The cold air slapped her face, waking her even more as she weaved through the garage. In her rush, the blanket slipped from her shoulders, falling into a crumpled heap on the floor. She barely noticed. It lay there, discarded, like a tangible sign of the chaos that had suddenly taken over her mind. But she couldn't stop. Her only focus was getting to the car, getting away, escaping the gnawing urgency that gripped her.

She climbed into her green Tahoe, her hands trembling as she grabbed the door handle.

The familiar creak of the door closing behind her felt distant, like something happening in another world. Without her glasses, her surroundings blurred at the edges, but that didn't matter either. She wasn't thinking about seeing clearly—she was thinking about leaving. Her fingers fumbled with the ignition, and the engine roared to life. She threw the car into reverse, backing out of the driveway without hesitation or a second thought. The early morning light filtered through the windshield, casting streaks of gold and shadow across the glass, distorting her already blurry vision. But she kept going, her heart pounding louder than the hum of the engine.

The road stretched out before her, long and empty, but her mind was anything but clear. Every turn of the wheel felt like it was being controlled by something outside of herself, a force that was pulling her further down the road. Her grip tightened as her breath came in shallow bursts. Confusion gnawed at her. Why was she driving? Where was she going? The questions didn't slow her down. She couldn't fight it, couldn't resist the pull that dragged her forward.

As she drove aimlessly, the familiar landscape passed by in a blur, her vision too fuzzy to make out the details. The trees lining the street were shadowy figures, houses mere smudges in the distance. Yet, something inside her started to shift, to focus. The fog in her mind thinned just enough for her to realize where she was being drawn. She was heading toward her ex-coworker's house. She didn't understand why, didn't know what had led her to that specific place, but the pull became undeniable. With every mile, every turn, she felt herself being led closer, as if an unseen hand was guiding her straight to their doorstep. It was out of her control now, as if the decision had been made long before she ever woke up that morning.

As Angelee recounted that night, there was a heaviness in her voice. A deep remorse mixed with a growing understanding of what happened. She's been learning about her illness, and now she realizes that what she did was during a schizophrenic episode—when reality and delusion blurred beyond recognition. Therapy and medication have helped her gain clarity, but that doesn't erase the weight of her actions.

Listening to her, I could see how much she has changed. The sister I once knew is still there, but now she's navigating a new reality. One where she understands the impact of her illness and the consequences of that tragic night. She carries the knowledge of what she's done, but now she's also working to live with it, gaining stability through the care she's receiving.

Nothing can change what happened, but Angelee's story, and her journey through mental illness, might bring awareness to others. It might help them recognize the signs before it's too late and remind us all how vital mental health support truly is.

THE FINAL CHAPTER: FINDING LIGHT IN THE SHADOWS

It's been over three years since that fateful day, and I still find myself wrestling with the weight of everything that's happened. Some days, the memories feel like a lifetime ago—like they belong to someone else's story. Other days, they're as fresh as if they happened yesterday, catching me off guard when I least expect it. But over time, I've learned to live with those moments, to let them pass without letting them consume me.

Angelee is in a place now where she's receiving the help she needs, and that brings me some peace. Her laughter, that warm, familiar sound, has returned, if only in glimpses. Seeing her smile reminds me of the girl I grew up with, the one who could brighten a room with that hearty laugh. It's a comfort, but also a reminder of all that's been lost along the way.

However, it's not just about loss anymore. It's about understanding. In the years since her diagnosis, I've come to realize that mental illness is a thief—a slow, methodical thief that robs people of their sense of self and their sense of reality. Often, it does so in silence, unseen by those closest to them until it's too late. I've replayed every conversation, every moment we shared, wondering if I or anyone could have done something different. But guilt doesn't change the past, and I've come to accept that sometimes, even when you're right next to someone, you can't see the battle they're fighting within.

Bill's family remains in my thoughts constantly. No matter how much time passes, I can never fully grasp the depth of their loss. I know that no apology, no amount of remorse or regret, will ever bring him back or ease the pain they carry. And that truth weighs heavy on my heart.

What I've come to realize is that there are some wounds time can't heal; wounds that stay with us, like scars, etched into the fabric of who we are.

Yet, despite everything, there's still hope. I've seen it in Angelee's eyes during our visits, in the way she's learning to navigate her illness with the help of her doctors and caregivers. I've seen it in the way she's beginning to take responsibility for her actions—not as the woman who was consumed by her delusions, but as the sister I've always known who's trying to find her way back to herself. And in that, I find a strange sense of reprieve.

In these past years, I've learned more about mental illness than I ever thought possible.

Schizophrenia is a monster that hides in the shadows, feeding on fear and isolation. But I've also learned that it's not invincible. With the right treatment, with compassion, and with the support of those around us, it can be managed. Not cured, but indeed managed. Angelee's story may be tragic, but it's not over.

For myself, the journey to healing is ongoing. I've stopped asking "why" so much—why this happened, why no one saw it coming—because there are no answers that will make sense of it. Instead, I've started to focus on "what now?" What can I do to ensure others don't suffer in silence? What can I do to make sure families don't find themselves in the same position as ours?

If there's one thing I've learned, it's that we must start paying attention to the quiet battles people are fighting. We need to talk about mental health openly, without shame or fear. We need to be willing to step in, even when it feels uncomfortable, even when we're not sure what to say or do. Angelee told me, in one of our most candid conversations, that what she needed most was for someone to pull her out before it was too late. "I wish someone had taken me to the hospital," she said. Those words echo in my mind every day.

The signs were there, hidden in plain sight, and we missed them. I'll live with that regret, but I refuse to let it paralyze me. Instead, I choose to use it as a reminder—to look closer, listen harder, and love more deeply. If sharing this story helps even one person, one family to take action sooner, then maybe some small good can come from all this pain.

This isn't about closing a chapter; it's about understanding and processing everything I've been through. The journey continues as I move forward. There will be days when the weight of it all feels unbearable, but there will also be days of hope. Days when I see Angelee smile, days when I feel the warmth of the sun on my face and know that, despite everything, there is still light in the world.

To Bill's family, I offer my deepest condolences and promise to never forget. To those reading this, I offer a plea: be there for the people you love. Pay attention, ask the hard questions, and don't wait until it's too late. And to those who are suffering in silence, I offer this: you are not alone. There is help, and there is hope.

This story is not one of redemption or happy endings. It's a story of survival—of trying, failing, and trying again. It's about finding peace, even when the world feels broken beyond repair. And while the wounds may never fully heal, I believe that, in time, we can learn to carry them with grace.

And with that, we exhale.

National Hotline for Mental Health Crises and Suicide Prevention

A toll-free hotline is available 24/7 and connects callers with a trained crisis counselor.

Call: 988

You can also text 988

1-800-273-TALK (8255)

ABOUT THE AUTHOR

Joe might work as an IT professional, but don't let that fool you—his passions go way beyond the monitors. He lives in Middle Tennessee with his wife, their two kids that are still at home, and Vanya, their Doberman who's fully convinced she's in charge. They have three adult children on their own out in the world. Joe spends his time finding balance between family life, travel, and creative projects. He's always ready for a new adventure, whether that's exploring a new culture, plotting the next family getaway, or mastering the art of minimalist packing of a carry-on bag.

When he's not on the move, you'll likely find Joe in his wood shop, surrounded by tools and sawdust, crafting something new from scratch. Building with his hands offers him a peaceful escape from his tech-filled world, and he takes pride in creating projects from the ground up.

Though Joe has always had a natural gift for spinning a good story, starting with fictional short stories he wrote just for fun, writing has recently become a way for him to reflect and connect with the world around him. With plenty of life experiences under his belt, he's full of stories waiting to be told. While he may not claim the title of "writer," one thing's for sure: there's a lot more coming from this guy.

Life's been a bit of an adventure for Joe. Whether he's at home or halfway across the globe, he's always ready for the next chapter. No matter where life takes him, he's constantly learning, growing, and finding new stories to tell along the way.

www.ingramcontent.com/pod-product-compliance
Lightning Source LLC
Chambersburg PA
CBHW062123040426
42337CB00044B/3831